WEDD

WIZN

Writing a
Great Resume

FAST FACTS
on Job Search Tools
and Techniques

for Those Seeking a New or Better Job,
More Career Opportunity, or a Fresh Start in Their Work

Peter Weddle

JUL   2006

ISBN: 1-928734-35-9

For more information about WEDDLE's and its publications,
Please visit our Web-site at
http://www.weddles.com.

Special discounts on bulk quantities of WEDDLE's books are available for libraries, corporations, professional associations and other organizations. For details, please contact WEDDLE's at 203.964.1888.

Special Thanks to Juliana, Meagan, Mikey and Joey.

WEDDLE's
www.weddles.com
2052 Shippan Avenue
Stamford, CT 06902
Where People Matter Most

"Restaurant patrons
looking for quality dining have Zagat.
For the recruitment industry,
the name is Weddle ...
Peter Weddle that is."

—American Staffing Association

What people are saying about WEDDLE's books and services:

As a Resource for Everyone:

"... a wealth of useful, updated information."

—*Library Journal*

"refreshingly unassuming and hype-free.... It's all excellent stuff...."

—Porter Anderson
CNN

"This book is a great resource.... It's like a travel guide to job boards."

—J.D.
BrassRing Systems

"WEDDLE's is the gorilla of knowledge and Web-sites when it comes to getting a job, managing human resources and recruiting on the Internet."

—Stone Enterprises, Ltd

As a Resource for Recruiters & HR Professionals:

"WEDDLE's is a very useful tool that recruiters and HR professionals will find helpful."

—*Fortune Magazine*

"The WEDDLE's Seminar has been held in cities around the country to rave reviews; in fact, more than 95% have said they found the seminars to be both very informative and very helpful."

—CareerJournal.com
from *The Wall Street Journal*

"When in doubt, consult WEDDLE's ... an industry standard."

—HRWIRE

"Peter Weddle's Wednesday post-conference session, "Internet Recruiting Strategy Update" was rated highest at our Staffing Industry Management Institute, as well as at last year's Staffing Industry Executive Forum. Typical was this comment, *'Gave me up-to-date, <u>now</u> information that I could use immediately'.*"

—Staffing Industry Report
Global Staffing Industry Report

". . . your newsletter is tremendously helpful to our recruiters. Keep up the fantastic work."

—S.W.
Harrahs

As a Resource for Job Seekers & Career Activists:

"The *WEDDLE's Job Seeker's Guide to Employment Web Sites* supplies clear, completely current information about each site's services, features and fees—helping users instantly determine which site best meets their needs. If you are looking for an objective guide to employment websites, ExecuNet recommends *WEDDLE's Guide.*"

—ExecuNet
The Center for Executive Careers

"Here's one of the best Web-sites to visit and refer to regarding job-hunting. Look into it first ... It'll provide you with a great competitive edge in the job market."

—S. B.,
Washington, D.C.

"Highly recommended!"

—Richard Nelson Bolles
author, *What Color Is You Parachute?*

Also by Peter Weddle

Career Fitness
A Vital Regimen for Building a Successful Work Life

CliffsNotes: Finding a Job on the Web

CliffsNotes: Writing a Great Resume

Computer-Based Instruction in Military Environments
(with Robert J. Seidel)

Electronic Resumes for the New Job Market

Generalship: HR Leadership in a Time of War

Internet Resumes: Take the Net to Your Next Job

Postcards From Space
Being the Best in Online Recruitment & HR Management
(2001, 2003)

The Hollow Enterprise
Why Investors in America's Companies Should Fear It;
Why the Leaders of America's Companies Must Fix It

'Tis of Thee
A Son's Search for the Meaning of Patriotism

WEDDLE's InfoNotes (WIN): Writing a Great Resume

WEDDLE's Recruiter's Guide to Employment Web Sites
(annually, 1999-2004)

WEDDLE's Job Seeker's Guide to Employment Web Sites
(annually, 2000-2004)

WEDDLE's Directory of Employment-Related Internet Sites
(annually, 2002-2004)

WEDDLE's Recruiter's Guide to Association Web Sites

CONTENTS

for
Job Seekers everywhere

Men and Women
who deserve the very best resources available
in their quest for career success

What is WEDDLE's?

WEDDLE's is a research, publishing, consulting and training firm specializing in HR leadership, employment, job search and career self-management.
Since 1996, WEDDLE's has conducted groundbreaking surveys of:

- recruiters and job seekers, *and*
- Web-sites providing employment-related services.

Our research and findings have been cited in such publications as *The Wall Street Journal*, *The New York Times*, and in *Money*, *Fortune*, and *Inc.* magazines.

WEDDLE's also publishes books, guides and directories that focus on organizations' acquisition and leadership of human capital and on individuals' achievement of their employment and career goals.
For recruiters and HR professionals, its publications include:

- *WEDDLE's bi-weekly e-Newsletter for Recruiters & HR Professionals* [FREE]
- *WEDDLE's Annual Guide to Employment Web Sites*
- *WEDDLE's Annual Directory of Employment-Related Internet Sites*
- *Postcards From Space: Being the Best in Online Recruitment & HR Management*
- *WEDDLE's Annual Guide to Association Web Sites*
- *The Keys to Successful Recruiting and Staffing*
- *Generalship: HR Leadership in a Time of War*
- *The Hollow Enterprise: Why Investors in America's Companies Should Fear It ... Why the Leaders of America's Companies Must Fix It*

For job seekers and career activists, its publications include:

- *WEDDLE's bi-weekly e-Newsletter for Job Seekers & Career Activists* [FREE]
- *WEDDLE's Annual Guide to Employment Web Sites*
- *WEDDLE's Annual Directory of Employment-Related Internet Sites*
- *WEDDLE's Annual Guide to Association Web Sites*
- *Career Fitness: A Vital Regimen for Building a Successful Work Life*
- *WizNotes: Fast Guides to Job Boards and Career Portals* with tailored guides for:

> Engineers,
> Sales & Marketing professionals,
> Finance & Accounting professionals,
> Human Resource professionals,
> Managers & Executives, and
> Recent College Graduates

- *WizNotes: Finding a Great Job on the Web*
- *WizNotes: Writing a Great Resume*

WEDDLE's also provides consultation to organizations in the areas of:

- HR leadership,
- Human capital formation,
- recruitment strategy development,
- employment brand positioning and communication,
- recruitment process reengineering and optimization, *and*
- Web-site design, development and implementation.

WEDDLE's delivers private seminars and workshops on the following subjects:

- Best Practices in Internet recruiting
  > for in-house corporate recruiters and managers
  > for staffing firm recruiters and managers

- Retention Strategies
  for managers and supervisors
- Human Resource leadership.

WHO IS PETER WEDDLE?

Peter Weddle is a former recruiter and business CEO turned author and speaker. He writes a bi-weekly column for CareerJournal.com from *The Wall Street Journal* and two newsletters that are distributed worldwide. Weddle has also authored or edited over twenty books and written numerous articles for leading magazines and journals. He has been cited in *The New York Times*, *The Washington Post*, *The Boston Globe*, *U.S. News & World Report*, *The Wall Street Journal*, *USA Today* and numerous other publications and has spoken to trade and professional associations and corporate meetings all over the world.

Introduction

In today's workplace, having a well-written resume that is always ready-to-go is an important part of your career planning. New and better jobs come and go at warp speed, and employment conditions change with little or no warning. An up-to-date resume that effectively describes your employment qualifications enables you to take full advantage of opportunities and weather the changes with less difficulty.

Your resume is a record of your work activities and accomplishments, organized and written to promote the contribution you can make on-the-job. It details your capabilities, emphasizes your strengths, and highlights the progress you've made in your career. If it's effective, your resume presents this information so that employers can assess—quickly and accurately—what you can do and how well you can do it.

This book shows you how to develop a resume that will highlight your qualifications for the job you want. It will help you select the best resume format for your employment situation and show you how to organize your skills and experience to the greatest advantage.

Why Do You Need This Book?

Can you answer yes to any of these questions?

- Do you need to learn how to write a powerful resume fast so that employers can recognize your capabilities and consider you for the jobs they have open right now?
- Do you not have the time to read a 500 page resume tome, but instead, want to choose the right information and format for your resume without wasting a lot of time on less-than-helpful details?
- Are you determined to make sure that your resume is properly designed to work with the computerized resume management systems now used by most employers?
- Are you about to graduate and need to know how to write a resume that can help you land a great first job?
- Do you want to be able to send your resume over the Internet to employers in your hometown and all over the world?

If so, then WEDDLE's WIZNotes: *Writing a Great Resume* is for you. It will show you how to write a resume that promotes your career success!

How to Use This Book

You're the boss here. You get to decide how to read this book. You can read it from cover-to-cover or you can skip around from chapter-to-chapter. If you want quick and easy access to a particular topic, you can:

- Use the Index in the back of the book to find what you're looking for.
- Flip through the book, looking for your topic in the Chapter and Section titles.
- Look for your topic in the Table of Contents in the front of the book.
- Look at the summary points highlighted at the beginning of each chapter in the section entitled IN THIS CHAPTER.
- Look for additional information in the WEDDLE's WIZNotes Resource Center or test your knowledge in the Review section.

Also, to find important information quickly, you can look for icons strategically placed throughout the text. These icons are designed to draw your attention to particularly important messages. They fall into the three categories described below.

Key Idea

If you see a Key Idea icon, make a mental note of this information—it's worth keeping in mind.

Helpful Hint

If you see a Helpful Hint icon, you'll know that you've run across a special tip, uncovered a little-known technique, or received some especially good advice.

Red Flag

The Red Flag icon alerts you to something that could undermine your resume's effectiveness and should, therefore, be avoided.

Don't Miss Our Web-Site

Keep up with the world of career management and resume writing by visiting the WEDDLE's Web-site at **http://www.weddles.com**. Here's what you find:

- The opportunity to sign up for a free, bi-weekly e-mail newsletter about the most effective job search techniques and career management strategies (see the sign up link beneath the spinning globe on our Home Page)
- A collection of tips on how to use the Internet to find a new or better job
- A directory of association Web-sites where you can network with others in your field
- A catalog of WEDDLE's books and other resources to help you win your dream job and manage your career successfully.

At www.weddles.com, you can even vote for your favorite employment Web-sites and see which sites won WEDDLE's User's Choice Awards last year. These sites are the best of the forty thousand job boards on the Internet, as selected by those who know best—the job seekers and recruiters who actually use them.

And if you haven't yet discovered how to put the Internet to work for your career, pick up a copy of WEDDLE's WIZNotes: *Finding a Job on the Web*. You'll learn just what you need to know to take the Information Superhighway to your next great job.

Chapter 1
Setting Expectations

IN THIS CHAPTER

- Understanding what your resume can do for you
- Meeting employers' needs
- Familiarizing yourself with the different types of resumes

Your resume is one your most important tools for finding and winning a great job. This one- to two-page document is both a record of your past and current accomplishments in the workplace and an advertisement for the capabilities you offer to other organizations, now and in the future. In effect, your resume describes what you can do and how well you can do it for an employer who has likely never met you before.

That information is critical to your success in today's job market. Employers are swamped with resumes from other job seekers, and only a well-written, high-impact resume can set you apart. It describes what makes you special by presenting a history of what you have achieved and a statement about the potential contribution you can make. A great resume will convincingly present your unique set of skills and experience on paper so that employers will invite you to an interview, where you can sell yourself in person. In short, a well-prepared resume gets you into the competition so that you have the chance to win your dream job.

Writing a resume can seem a bit intimidating, whether you're a first-time job seeker or a seasoned workplace veteran, a skilled technician or a senior executive. The process is, however, something anyone can accomplish, and everyone should. Yes, it will take a little time and effort; but no, you do not need a degree in English or a background in career counseling to prepare an effective resume. Creating a great resume simply requires careful preparation, attention to detail, selection of the right type of resume for your work background and objective, and thorough follow-through. Do those things, and you'll produce a resume that can open the door to exciting new work opportunities and position you for continuous career advancement.

UNDERSTANDING WHAT YOUR RESUME CAN DO FOR YOU

A great resume can help you accomplish two important objectives. It will present your work credentials in such a way that you:

- Qualify to compete for open jobs of interest to you in the near future
- Are effectively positioned for career-enhancing positions in the mid-to-longer term.

Making a positive first impression

In today's fast-changing workplace, a great resume is one of the key components of success. It acts as your agent, a tireless advocate for your career interests and goals. If you're job hunting, your resume is the means by which you introduce yourself to employers and networking contacts. It is the document you use to establish your credentials when applying for a position and to describe your background and goals when prospecting for job leads.

In most cases, your resume gives employers their first look at you. The document's content, clarity, and persuasiveness—as much as the actual details of your career record and work credentials—will determine whether that first impression is positive and helpful or not. And making a positive first impression has never been more important in the job market. Research shows that employers typically spend just 15 to 45 seconds reviewing each resume they receive. That's all the time your resume has to convey your qualifications for an open position. The quality and impact of that initial impression will determine whether you are considered for the position . . . or rejected out-of-hand.

First impressions can also have a significant impact on your networking. Connecting with others to uncover job leads is an important part of any successful job search campaign. In many cases, you will be meeting people for the first time, and your resume will help shape their impression of you. A great resume that creates a positive initial impression can expand the range of people who are willing to meet with you and point you toward interesting employment opportunities.

Protecting your career

Even if you're not actively job hunting, a great resume can help you achieve career success. In fact, it can be a very effective tool for protecting yourself against unforeseen employment disruptions and minimizing their impact on your career advancement.

Today, employment security largely depends on three key steps that only you can take:

- Your efforts to keep your occupational skills and knowledge up-to-date;
- Your readiness to begin a job search campaign on a moment's notice should you need to do so; and
- Your ability to expand your circle of contacts continuously so that your capabilities are widely known among employers.

Let's explore each of these steps in a bit more detail.

STAYING UP-TO-DATE. In a demanding business environment, your value to current and future employers is directly dependent on the how deep and current your occupational skills and knowledge are. Half of that expertise grows obsolete every 3–5 years, however, due to technological and other changes. As a consequence, you now must *continuously replenish and improve your credentials* to keep your career healthy and moving forward.

Despite its importance, this requirement for lifelong learning sometimes slips in its position among our priorities. The demands of today's job can mask the need for continuous self-improvement and preparation for the future. That's where your resume can help. It's a record of your personal development, in the present as well as the past, and that makes it an effective tool for measuring your progress in developing your work skills. In other words, if you don't have to update your resume every six months or so—to document newly acquired capabilities or experience—odds are good that your career is falling behind—a fitting reminder that you need to invest more time and energy in personal development.

⇒◎ *Helpful Hint*

Schedule a "personal performance appraisal" with yourself every six months. Use your resume to evaluate your progress in the previous six- month period and to set clear, achievable goals for the next.

STAYING READY. Having an up-to-date resume is also important because it ensures that you are *ready and able to initiate a job search campaign at a moment's notice.* Despite laws requiring advance notice, employer staff reductions, downsizing and restructuring actions can occur suddenly and without warning. Those who begin prospecting for re-employment first have a real and powerful competitive advantage in the job market.

In addition, new and exciting career opportunities may come along at any moment. Not surprisingly, the competition for such positions is fierce, and they seldom stay open for long. Being able to respond in a timely fashion can be an important factor in winning that dream job you've always wanted.

STAYING CONNECTED. A great resume can also help you promote your credentials to others. Traditionally, cultivating that kind of connection was something you did only in an active job search. In today's ever-changing workplace, however, marketing your credentials should be a continuous activity. It is the best way to develop the contacts who can help you manage your career proactively.

In the past, this networking was limited to who you knew; today, it's based on who knows you as well as who you know. While face-to-face meetings remain as important as always, it's also essential that you connect with people in other ways, as well. The more contacts you have who are aware of what you can do and how well you can do it, the greater the prospects for advancing your career.

Your resume enables you to provide an accurate, up-to-date, and upbeat introduction to your track record on-the-job, so that you can extend the circle of people who know you. That ever-expanding network of contacts who are aware of your capabilities in the workplace helps ensure that you are considered for as many opportunities as possible and thus have a range of options to consider as you manage your career.

MEETING EMPLOYERS' NEEDS

Recruiters use resumes to identify prospective candidates for their open positions and to screen candidates to select the best qualified for further consideration and interviewing.

Providing the information employers need to select qualified candidates

Most employers use several methods to locate qualified candidates for an open position. They may advertise in newspapers or other print publications, post their jobs at their own site on the Internet as well as on those operated by commercial recruitment companies, network with colleagues in other organizations, hire a staffing firm or retain an executive search firm. Whatever the approach, the information they acquire about candidates typically arrives in a paper, electronic or Internet resume. Although many organizations also use application forms, resumes remain the most widely used document among employers seeking to identify candidates for a position vacancy.

An employer's initial assessment of a resume usually involves one or more reviews to determine how closely the person described in the document matches the profile of an ideal candidate. In most cases, the information provided in the resume about a person's field of employment, experience, and skills is compared to the requirements specified in a position description or recruiting requisition developed by the organization's Human Resource Department and/or the hiring manager for the opening.

Often, a quick evaluation is performed first to eliminate those individuals who clearly are not qualified for the position because they have no background in the requisite career field or lack adequate experience. Then, a much more detailed assessment is performed to identify those candidates who best match the position specifications and should, therefore, be interviewed by telephone and/or in person.

To best represent you in this evaluation process, your resume must present your qualifications in the right vocabulary and in the right place.

THE RIGHT VOCABULARY. Recruiters look for terms that express the skills and knowledge required to qualify a candidate for the open job. Because most recruiters do not have a working background in the technical fields for which they recruit, the greater the similarity between the terms they use and the terms found in your resume, the easier it is for a match to be identified. Therefore, *express your qualifications in the vocabulary of recruiters.*

➥◎ *Helpful Hint*

To determine the exact words and phrases to use in your resume, check the employment ads in your local newspaper and other publications for positions similar to the one you're seeking. See how recruiters are describing your skills and background, and then, include their terms in your resume.

THE RIGHT PLACE. The sheer volume of resumes that employers must review for each position precludes them from spending more than a moment or two on each document. In such a situation, even qualified candidates can be overlooked if their skills and experience are hard to find in the body of their resumes. To make sure your resume isn't missed for the position you want, *summarize your credentials in a paragraph entitled "Profile" and place it at the top of your resume,* just above the Experience section. Although other sections of your resume will provide much more information about your capabilities, this up-front summary ensures that even a harried reviewer can quickly find and evaluate your potential match with an open position.

Understanding how employers process resumes

Today, resumes can follow one of two paths when they are received and processed by employers.

When you send your resume by mail or fax to an employer's Human Resource Department, the document goes through several steps:

1. The employer quickly reviews the resume to assess its match with the requirements for a specific open position and/or the employer's general hiring needs. If no match is possible (for example, you're a pastry chef and the organization manufactures surf boards), you will likely not be notified, and your resume will be immediately discarded. If, on the other hand, your resume demonstrates the possibility of a match, you may or may not be notified, but it will proceed on to the next step.

2. In most cases, your resume will next be entered into a computerized resume management system. Employers now receive so many resumes from prospective candidates that even small and mid-sized organizations have turned to these systems to help them organize and use candidate information. Basically, a resume management system enables an employer to store the contents of your resume in a database where it can be subsequently located for further review.

    If your resume is not entered into a computer, it will normally be stored in a traditional paper-based filing system. In most cases, the original of your resume will remain in its file in the Human Resource Department for a specified period of time (in many cases, 6-12 months). When recruiters or hiring managers want to review the document, copies are made and distributed, as necessary.

=•◎ *Helpful Hint*

Because most organizations use copies rather than the original of your resume for internal distribution, produce your resume on high-grade white paper. Only the copy shop appreciates your use of more expensive colored paper, and worse, doing so can adversely affect the clarity of subsequent photocopies.

3. If you're applying for a specific position, your resume will also be subjected to a detailed review to assess your qualifications for that opening. If there appears to be a good match, you may be called by a recruiter who will conduct a telephone interview to obtain additional information (for example, your availability date or your willingness to travel, if that's a requirement of the position) and further evaluate your credentials.

4. The resumes of the best-qualified candidates are then sent, either electronically (through the resume management system) or by paper, to the hiring manager for review. Based on that evaluation, a decision is made about whether or not to invite you in for a face-to-face interview. If you receive an invitation, your resume will probably be used to develop and organize the questions you will be asked (for example, to obtain more information about certain key areas of your background or to clear up an inconsistency in your employment record). If you do not receive an invitation, your resume will be returned to the resume management or paper filing system so that it can be considered for future openings.

When you send your resume over the Internet to an employer or attach it to an online application form, the e-document goes through several steps:

1. Your resume travels through cyberspace as e-mail. In many (but definitely not all) cases, the employer will notify you of its receipt in a return e-mail message and describe what will happen next.

   • Some employers will quickly review your resume to assess its applicability to a specific opening or to the organization's general hiring needs. Those deemed potentially qualified will be routed into the employer's resume management system. Those resumes deemed not qualified are normally deleted, often without any notification to you.

- Other employers do not review the resumes they receive over the Internet and simply route the resume into their resume management system for storage.

2. If your resume is reviewed and deemed potentially qualified for a specific opening, the computer file will be flagged for further evaluation. If your resume is not reviewed, it can only be identified for a particular opening when a recruiter searches the database of the resume management system and identifies it as a match with the candidate criteria specified for the opening. Whichever course your resume takes, once it is identified as potentially appropriate for a specific position, it will be subjected to a de-tailed analysis. As in the paper resume process, you may then be called by a recruiter who will conduct a telephone interview to obtain additional information and further evaluate your credentials.

3. The resumes of the best-qualified candidates are sent electronically through the resume management system to the hiring manager for review. From that point on, the process proceeds exactly as it does for a paper resume. A decision is made about whether to invite you in for a face-to-face interview. If you receive an invitation, your resume will likely be used to develop and organize the questions you will be asked. If you do not receive an invitation, your resume is returned to the resume management system so that it can be considered for future openings.

DESCRIBING DIFFERENT STYLES & FORMATS OF RESUMES

You can choose to create your resume in any of three styles and pick from three alternative formats for their presentation. The three styles of resumes are chronological, functional, and hybrid. The three alternative formats are paper, electronic and Internet.

The chronological resume

A chronological resume describes your work experience as history. It is structured around dates, employers and titles, beginning with your most recent job and working backward to your first position in the workplace. This format enables you to demonstrate a steady progression of your work skills and responsibilities. On the other hand, this resume type also focuses the reader's attention on what you have done, rather than on what you can do. Indeed, the chronological resume is often described as the "obituary resume" because it is the perfect format for writing a summary of your worklife.

Chronological resumes are the most prevalent type of resume in circulation today—for many reasons. First, this account of your employment past is easier for you to write than either a functional or hybrid resume. It has a logical structure and requires information that you are likely to have readily at hand. Second, the chronological resume also makes the recruiter's job easier. It formats your experience so that it can be quickly and accurately compared to the requirements for an open position and provides a reasonable structure for a follow-up interview.

The functional resume

A functional resume is a description of what you can do, arranged according to how well you can do it. Its organizing principle is your capabilities, not a chronology of your experience. In effect, a functional resume leads with your strength by focusing on your skills and abilities, regardless of when you applied them in your career. The details of your employment history are included only to the extent that they illustrate your functional expertise.

Functional resumes are not as popular as chronological resumes. They are more difficult to write and are not as easily understood by recruiters. They require that you organize the presentation of your career information by the contribution you can make to a future employer rather than by what you did for an employer in the past. Further, they are more difficult for recruiters to evaluate because they do not present your career in a traditional linear format. Nevertheless, functional resumes can be particularly effective in describing your qualifications if you are entering the workforce for the first time and don't have a long track record of work experience or if there are gaps in your work history—for child rearing, education, or even to take time off—and therefore can't demonstrate an unbroken record of employment experience.

The hybrid resume

The hybrid resume, also called the "combination resume," attempts to bring together the best elements of both the chronological and functional formats. It includes a brief history of your work record and a detailed description of your functional qualifications. Typically, you position the work history section before the presentation of your qualifications so that recruiters can quickly scan and evaluate your experience on-the-job. The only exception to this arrangement is if you are a first-time job seeker without a lengthy occupational record. In that case, place your work history section after the presentation of your qualifications.

Hybrid resumes are as difficult to write as functional resumes. Moreover, the addition of a work history section consumes space on your resume and can force you to cut information in order to keep the document to a length that employers will accept. Further, the use of two experience sections can cause overlap and redundancy in the information that you do present. Nevertheless, this format provides almost everything a recruiter needs to evaluate your credentials: a summary of your past work record plus a detailed description of the skills and abilities you can offer to a future employer.

The paper resume

Despite some breathless predictions in the media, the paper resume is neither extinct nor about to fall into disuse. While it is true that some organizations will now only accept resumes submitted via the Internet, the vast majority of employers continue to welcome paper resumes. However, always follow the instructions employers provide in their employment advertising, even if that means submitting your resume over the Internet rather than on paper. On the other hand, if the employer is willing to accept a paper resume, make sure that yours is formatted for the electronic environment in today's Human Resource Departments.

The electronic resume

The electronic resume or e-resume is a special format designed for the technology-based processing equipment prevalent in Human Resource Departments today. Many employers now rely on computerized resume management systems to store and organize the resumes they receive from candidates. These systems require that your paper resume be converted into information that a computer can accept and use. The conversion is accomplished with a device called a scanner. Scanners are very sensitive, however, and cannot process many of the standard features used in word processed documents. Therefore, the only way you can ensure that your resume will be accurately included in such systems is to reconfigure it to make the document "computer-friendly."

Electronic resumes involve adjustments to both the format and content of your resume. To help scanners "read" your resume, you have to eliminate all of the underlining, italics, graphics, and other conventions you have used to structure and highlight your information. In addition, to help the computer find your resume in its database, you have to augment its content with "keywords" that describe your background and skills. Finally, you have to take certain precautions in producing your resume to avoid other problems that can affect its accurate processing into a resume management system. (For complete instructions on developing an e-resume, please see Chapter 8.)

The Internet resume

A growing number of employers are now using the Internet to acquire resumes from candidates. They post their open positions on their own Web-sites and on commercial recruitment sites and even ask that responses to print advertisements be sent to a designated e-mail address. When you use the Internet to apply for these openings or to transmit your resume, you gain the advantage of speed. Your credentials arrive at the employer's Human Resource Department where they can be processed and evaluated while the resumes of other job seekers are still working their way through the traditional postal system.

When you send your resume over the Internet, it usually travels in the body of an e-mail message. However, the software programs used to send e-mail do not normally transmit traditional word processed documents accurately. The journey through cyberspace tends to garble their contents, rendering them unintelligible to the recipient. To use the Internet effectively, therefore, you must re-configure your resume for online transmission. This adjustment involves converting it to plain unformatted text and narrowing the margins of the document to a maximum of 65 characters. In addition, you must eliminate any Greek, mathematical and business symbols that appear in the body of your resume. (For complete instructions on developing an Internet resume or i-resume, please see Chapter 9.)

 ### *Red Flag*

Unless the employer specifically asks you to, do *not* send your resume as an attachment to an e-mail message. Many computer viruses are transmitted in attachments, so most Human Resource Departments are now reluctant to open them. So, how should you send your resume over the Internet? Copy and paste it into the body of an e-mail message.

Chapter 2
Learning the Basics

IN THIS CHAPTER

- Creating a resume with the right stuff
- Assembling the seven core elements of a great resume
- Debunking the myths about writing and using resumes

All great resumes embody features and principles that enable them to serve both your interests and those of recruiters. When they are well written, these documents clearly and emphatically communicate who you are—your personality, work habits, and work style—as well as what you can do in the workplace and the great ways you can do it.

RECOGNIZING THE HALLMARKS OF A GREAT RESUME

A great resume has four distinguishing features. Each of these features contributes to a positive first impression—in written form—-and all of them are necessary if your resume is to have that effect.

A great resume sells your successes

A great resume promotes you as an employment candidate by highlighting your capabilities and accomplishments. It focuses on the successes you have enjoyed at work and the contributions you have made to other employers. Your resume is not the place to volunteer negative information; if there is a potentially negative aspect of your record, you should, of course, provide a complete and accurate accounting, but only in an interview and only if asked.

To be effective, your resume should describe the tasks you performed, the actions you took, and the benefits you delivered. For greater impact, use clear, persuasive statements in the active voice (for example, "I identified and sold new accounts nationwide.") rather than dull sounding responsibility statements (for example, "I was responsible for developing and selling new accounts nationwide.") Such a well-crafted presentation portrays you as a person who gets the job done, rather than as someone who simply filled a job description.

Some people are uncomfortable with proactively selling themselves. Pointing out your finest qualities is, however, the best way to set yourself and your record apart. Selling your successes tells an employer that you understand what he or she is looking for and explains, how—if hired—you are likely to perform on-the-job. Although you may feel as if you're boasting, you're not. As the old saying notes, "It ain't braggin' if ya' done it."

Great resumes tell the truth

A great resume is accurate and truthful. It portrays your employment record in the best possible light, but never by making misleading statements, fudging the facts, or exaggerating your role or accomplishments. Employers know that many resumes contain false information. As a result, they are now much more vigilant about checking employment dates, positions held, activities performed, and other details presented on resumes. And nothing will end your candidacy for that dream job more quickly than to be caught up in a lie. So, don't risk it; rely on just the facts—without embellishment.

A great resume is error-free

A great resume also has no spelling, grammatical, or typographical errors. It is neat, well-written, and carefully edited. Such a resume gives employers two ways of looking at you: First, it provides the information they need to evaluate your employment record; and second, it affords them an insight into what you are like as a worker. An error-free resume demonstrates that you are a careful person who is attentive to detail and have pride in what you do.

A great resume is clear and complete, but concise

A great resume provides everything an employer needs to evaluate your qualifications for a position opening. Being complete, however, doesn't mean drowning the reader in a tidal wave of marginally helpful information. A great resume is never more than two pages long. Leave out any irrelevant details or facts that do not substantially enhance your employment credentials. In addition, present your information in short, hard-hitting statements that are easy-to-read and understand. Avoid flowery or pretentious language, run-on sentences, and long-winded paragraphs.

PRACTICING THE PRINCIPLES OF WRITING A GREAT RESUME

Every great resume has seven core elements, all of which must be present for it to be complete and effective:

- Contact information
- Objective
- Profile
- Experience
- Accomplishments
- Education
- Professional Affiliations & Awards

Without these core elements, most recruiters will consider a resume incomplete and often discard it.

In addition, these core elements should appear on your resume in the order shown above. The only exception is on the resumes of first-time job seekers. If you're looking for your first job after graduating from high school or college, change the order of the elements as follows: Contact information, Objective, Profile, Education, Experience, Accomplishments and Professional Affiliations & Awards. (Please see Chapter 7 for additional information on the resumes of first-time job seekers.) For all others, the resume layout on the next page shows the organization of each element as it should appear over one or two pages.

Contact information

Begin your resume by centering your name at the top of the first page. Use your complete name, but not any informal or nickname or such designations as Mr., Ms., or Mrs.. In addition, do not give the document a title, such as "Resume" or "The Resume of John Doe."

Beneath your name, position your postal address, telephone number, and e-mail address, if you have one. This information is critically important as it enables employers and recruiters to contact you for additional details and, potentially, to schedule an interview.

Your Name

Contact Information   Contact Information
Contact Information   Contact Information

OBJECTIVE

_____

_____

PROFILE

_____

_____

EXPERIENCE

First entry

_____

_____

_____

_____

_____

- Accomplishment
- Accomplishment

Second entry

_____

_____

_____

_____

_____

- Accomplishment
- Accomplishment

EDUCATION

_____

_____

PROFESSIONAL AFFILIATIONS & AWARDS

_____

_____

➳◎ *Helpful Hint*

If possible, provide a telephone number where you can be reached privately during the business day. Otherwise, use a private telephone number that will be answered by another adult, a voice mail service, or an answering machine. Then, make sure that you check your messages regularly and return recruiters' calls promptly. Similarly, use a private e-mailbox—not one provided by your employer (which is subject to inspection)—to receive e-mail from recruiters. Check your incoming e-mail at least twice daily.

Objective

Your Objective statement tells the employer what kind of position you're seeking and helps you to organize your resume. Place this single sentence, which generally runs about 20–30 words, just below your contact information. (For guidelines on writing an effective Objective statement, please see Chapter 3.)

Profile

A Profile appears below your objective statement and summarizes your key skills, abilities, experience, and knowledge. It is roughly the same length as an Objective statement and written in 3-5 bullets or short descriptive phrases.

☯➠ *Key Idea*

A Profile functions as a billboard that highlights your strengths in the workplace, and by being positioned near the top of your resume, enables recruiters to assess your qualifications quickly and accurately. Its content should be rich with keywords—the nouns and phrases that recruiters use to describe qualifications similar to yours. Review the terms they include in their recruitment ads, job postings on the Internet, and position descriptions, if you have access to them. Then, write your Profile with recruiters' vocabulary, always ensuring that the information you include is accurate, clearly expressed, and persuasive. For example:

PROFILE

- 15 years of experience as a successful sales agent in the personal insurance industry

- Top performer in the Eastern Region for the past five years
- Experienced at both new account sales and current account management and growth

Experience

The Experience section provides a detailed description of your work credentials. Because both the space on your resume and the time recruiters have to review it are limited, include information that clearly and directly supports your Objective. Each detail should be designed to provide evidence of your skills and knowledge, your track record in applying those attributes on-the-job, and your potential to extend that capability into another organization and a new position. If you use a chronological or hybrid style of resume, this section will also detail your previous employers, positions held, and locations. (Please see Chapter 1 for a description of chronological and hybrid resumes.)

In today's job market, employers are seeking very specific kinds of talent. They want to hire individuals who have demonstrated high levels of performance in their occupational fields and gained the kind of experience that would prepare them to achieve similar success in the future. Therefore, your Experience section should provide a focused, hard-hitting summary of what you can do, not who you hope to be. It is a place for fact, not dreams; achievable objectives, not wishful thinking.

Accomplishments

In most cases, your accomplishments are best presented as bullets in your Experience section. These mini-success stories provide two kinds of information to employers.

First, they are the details that prove how capable you are in your occupational field. Because quantitative measures are often easiest to understand and have the greatest impact on the reader, describing your on-the-job achievements in numbers, rather than phrases, may attract the most employer attention. Here's an example:

- Increased sales by 30% in just two years
- Accomplished special project on time and within budget, producing a $150,000 profit for the company
- Managed a weather-related spike of 5,000 claims within 60 days by hiring and training five new employees

Second, your accomplishments also provide employers with information about your character. These glimpses into proven performance are a statement about the pride you take in your work. They describe your sense of commitment to making genuine contributions on-the-job. And they are a measure of the importance you attach to being the best you can be in your profession, craft, or trade.

Education

Your resume also presents your most important education and training credentials. Once again, what you say in your Objective should determine what you include in this section. Cite past programs in which you pursued a degree and any curricula in which you are currently involved.

☞ *Key Idea*

Today, employers look very favorably on candidates who recognize the importance of and take responsibility for keeping their skills current. Therefore, think of yourself as a work-in-progress; always be enrolled in a program that extends your skills and knowledge in the workplace and always include that information on your resume.

The Education section of your resume should include the following information:

- The name of the degree(s) or certificate(s) you have earned or are earning
- The specific field in which you majored or the subject you are currently studying
- The institution where you did or are now doing your coursework
- The date your degree(s)/certificate(s) were awarded or the term "Ongoing," if you have not yet completed the program

For example:

BS/Software Engineering Carnegie Mellon, Pittsburgh, PA 1971

JAVA Programming University of Connecticut, Storrs, CT On-going

Professional Affiliations & Awards

In the Professional Affiliations & Awards section, cite the names of any professional societies or associations to which you belong, as well as any positions you have held, presentations you have delivered at annual or chapter meetings, and articles you have authored for publication. Don't include the citation you received for helping out at the local community center, but do highlight any activities or achievements that underscore your dedication to your field and demonstrate your improved competency. For example:

- Member, American Marketing Association, 1975–Present
- President, Mid-Ohio Chapter—American Marketing Association, 1991-93
- "Building Powerful Brands" paper presented at American Marketing Association 9th Annual Convention, 1998

DISPELLING RESUME MYTHS

Myths are plentiful on the subject of writing and using a resume. By avoiding the mistakes that misleading information can cause, you will create a more powerful resume and achieve more gratifying results with the document you have written.

Ten common misperceptions about writing a great resume

To put together a resume that will attract the kind of attention you seek and express to an employer the qualifications that count, you need to consider the following stumbling blocks—any one of which can trip you up as you travel along your career path.

1. **Resumes are easy to write and can be completed quickly.** This view has long been prevalent among those who ignore their resumes until that panicked moment when they have to begin an active job search. The truth, however, is that writing an effective resume requires both time and effort. Anyone can do it, but it takes intensive self-assessment, careful preparation, and detailed execution—often with several revisions—to produce a well crafted docu-

ment. The return on that investment is a resume that will serve you well in the job market and help you manage your career successfully.

2. **Once, written, your resume need not be updated or tailored.** Your resume is actually a living document. It should be constantly updated and refined to reflect your own growth and development in the workplace. Continued refinement can help you gauge your career progress and ensure that your record is always ready and available for review, should an attractive opportunity become available.

3. **Page count doesn't matter.** Unfortunately, it does. Employers have limited time to review your resume and limited space in which to store it. Therefore, keep your resume to two pages maximum and use your Objective statement to focus on the information that will best position you to compete for the kind of job you want.

➛◎ *Helpful Hint*

To make sure that an employer will correctly enter your resume into a computerized resume management system (Please see Chapter 1), print each page on a separate sheet of paper, rather than on both sides of the same sheet.

4. **The best resume identifies your previous responsibilities.** Employers are less interested in responsibilities than in work accomplished—what you did and how well you did it—in previous jobs. Therefore, use action verbs to describe the tasks you performed, the actions you took and the achievements you accomplished. For example, "Performed daily audits of all accounts payable activities. Corrected errors and updated records to ensure compliance with internal policy and external regulations. Trained new clerks and oversaw their initial work."

5. **Your resume should state your salary expectations.** Your resume is not the place to make salary demands. Stating a salary requirement simply adds another concern that may cause an employer to reject you as a candidate. Therefore, focus your resume on presenting your credentials in such a clear and compelling way

that an employer will voluntarily make you a generous job offer and keep any compensation-related talks to a minimum.

6. **Your resume should include references and personal information.** A recruiter expects you to be able to provide references when asked, so there's no reason to state "References available on request" or to note references' names and contact information on your resume. Also, do not include such personal information as your gender, age, ethnic background, marital status, religion, and height and weight (unless it is relevant to performing the job you're seeking).

7. **Your resume should state why you left your previous position or are leaving your current one.** This issue is likely to come up during your evaluation by a recruiter, but it is best addressed in an interview, rather than on your resume. Moreover, when providing such information, always avoid making critical statements regarding your previous employers and co-workers. Negative remarks can cause recruiters to worry about what you would say should you leave their organization.

8. **Your resume should include a recent photograph.** Employers must avoid any discrimination based on a person's ethnicity, gender, age, or religion. A photograph can inadvertently lead to such a situation, so most employers do not want to see them on a resume.

9. **Your resume should includes lots of graphics and art work to make it eye-appealing.** Making your resume attractive is important, but complex graphics and even overly elaborate typefaces (such as Old English) take up space and make it difficult for your resume to be processed by computerized resume management systems. The best way to highlight the information in your resume is to provide plenty of white space on the document. Using bullets and short paragraphs of no more than 4–5 lines will break up your text and set off important details.

10. **You can write a great resume by simply filling in the blanks.** Avoid using "plug and chug" templates when writing your resume. These canned programs are available in software, on CDs, and in print workbooks. Their generic language and cookie-cutter look and feel are

easily recognized by recruiters and undercut the impact of your resume.

Three common misperceptions about using a resume

Although not as common as the myths about resume writing, there are a number of misconceptions about how to use a resume effectively in a job search.

1. **You don't need a resume to get a job.** Although every rule has its exceptions, a resume is normally your ticket into the job market. Recruiters are under intense pressure to locate and interview candidates and fill open positions quickly. If you don't have a resume, you slow down the evaluation process and increase the recruiter's risk of making a hiring mistake. Moreover, not having such an important document can create the perception that you don't take adequate responsibility for your career, and that view, in turn, can raise a red flag about your suitability for the job.

2. **Your resume will get you a job.** Only *you* can get you a job. A great resume should intrigue employers so much that they want to meet with you. In other words, your resume can open an employer's door—giving you the opportunity to sell yourself—but after that, it's up to you. A resume is an integral part of a larger process that involves research, follow-up, and additional communications, all of which you must plan and execute effectively to achieve your job search objective.

3. **How you send your resume to a recruiter doesn't matter.** The way you send your resume to an employer has an impact on its effectiveness when a recruiter is reviewing the document. For example, don't mail your resume folded into a typical #10 business envelope. Instead, send the pages in a 9-inch-x-12-inch envelope unfolded so that they can be properly processed by the computerized resume management systems now being used in most employers' Human Resource Departments. Similarly, a resume sent over the Internet should be formatted and adjusted to ensure its accurate transmission via e-mail. (For additional information on resume distribution, please see Chapters 8 and 9.)

NOTES

Chapter 3
Creating a Great Resume

IN THIS CHAPTER

- Taking the first step
- Expressing your Objective in a statement
- Pinpointing the right style of resume for you

The key to creating a great resume is to understand what you want the document to achieve for you and to select the best style of resume for accomplishing that goal.

TAKING THE FIRST STEP

The first step in writing an effective resume is to determine your employment Objective.

Setting your sights

Great resumes have a clear and unambiguous theme. Every detail that is included in the resume supports that theme and reinforces its impact on the reader. This theme is your Objective; it has two elements:

- The opportunity and circumstances you are looking for in your next job
- A clear and positive relationship to your career and its advancement

In other words, your Objective has both a near-term and a mid-to-longer term purpose. The message you're conveying focuses on your immediate goal in the job market—to make very clear the kind of job, work, and employer you're seeking. Your Objective also connects your past, current, and future jobs into an integrated strategy and direction for your career.

Determining your Objective requires that you know what interests you professionally and what potential positions will allow you to express those interests. In addition, you need a realistic sense of your current skill level and expertise in a chosen field. You can then determine the level and scope of position for which you are competitive. Achieving such understanding involves both introspection and research. You must know yourself and the workplace and continually update that knowledge as you grow and develop, and the workplace changes.

⇒◎ *Helpful Hint*

Taking stock of your interests and making sure that they are aligned with your work is necessary whether you're a first-time job seeker, a seasoned worker at mid-career, or a highly paid expert in your field. Only you can direct your career—not your employer, a teacher or even a well meaning friend—and thoughtful, well informed career management is the only way to achieve real and lasting success in the workplace.

To help you with the process of self-exploration, use one or both of the following exercises.

THE LOTTERY. Imagine that you have won a huge jackpot in the lottery. Suddenly, finances are no longer an issue. The mortgage is paid, money is put away for the kids' educations, and your retirement program is generously funded. Now, you can do whatever you want to do with your life's work. What would that be? What activity would get you up in the morning and give you the most satisfaction at the end of the day? Describe it in a few lines—either on paper or in an electronic document that you can refer to.

YOUR TOMBSTONE. You spend much of your life at work. Aside from your family, faith, and friends, your career is probably the most important aspect of your life. If you suddenly learned that you were terminally ill, how would you like to be remembered? What would you be most proud of having accomplished at work? What would give you the greatest satisfaction? Write your thoughts down.

If you're a first-time job seeker, you may have to research which occupations and specific jobs provide the opportunity to express these interests and motivated abilities. If you are a seasoned workplace veteran who is in transition or seeking greater satisfaction in your work, you may need to explore alternative career fields. Whatever your situation, you can find such information at college and university career centers, state employment security offices, public libraries, and on the Internet. For example, America's Job Bank (www.ajb.dni.us) offers a Career InfoNet that can help you identify career paths and opportunities. So too can professional career counselors who have the appropriate training and experience to guide adult workers.

Getting help

If you need help in pinpointing your career interest, you can find several assessment instruments available through professional career counselors and centers. These include the following:

- The Myers-Briggs Type Indicator
- The Keirsey Temperament Test
- The Self-Directed Search (SDS)
- The Unisex Edition of the ACT Interest Inventory (UNIACT)
- The Vocational Interest Inventory (VII)
- The Career Occupational Preference System Interest Inventory (COPS)

EXPRESSING YOUR OBJECTIVE IN A STATEMENT

Creating a statement that will serve as your employment Objective not only helps focus your resume, but also keeps your career on track by providing a clear direction toward an outcome that represents success for you. In addition, you can rephrase your Objective statement so that it tailors your goals and capabilities to the needs of specific employers and thus make yourself a more attractive employment candidate.

Organizing your Objective statement

Your objective statement should express two important considerations:

- Your desired outcome—the specific kind of work that you want to do
- The context in which you want to do it—the title or description of a specific position

The statement should also indicate the kind of organization in which you want to be employed and the benefit you will provide to that organization through the application of your skills. The more specific you can be, the better. Vague Objective statements often lead to unfocused resumes that do not present a clear, hard-hitting message about your capabilities and interests.

Organize the information in your Objective statement as follows:

Title or description of your desired job + the kind of organization for which you want to work + the benefit you will convey to the organization.

For example:

OBJECTIVE

A store manager position for a leader in the men's retail clothing industry where I can use my team-building skills and sales experience to increase store revenue and profits.

Writing your Objective statement

Use the following four-step process to write your Objective statement.

1. Identify or confirm the kind of position that will best enable you to express and develop your motivated skills and abilities. Describe the position or note its title in a few words.
2. Identify the context or organizational setting in which you most enjoy working. Do you prefer a high risk/high reward start-up organization, an established industry leader, an entrepreneurial culture, or some other kind of organization? Describe the context you seek in a phrase.
3. Determine the key experience and skills you will bring to your new employer. Identify capabilities that will underscore the contribution you can make to its success. Make a list of those benefits.
4. Integrate the results of Steps 1–3 into a clear and concise Objective statement. Write out that statement.

Locating your Objective statement

☸⧽ *Key Idea*

When you send your resume to a prospective employer, make sure that your Objective statement appears in the body of your resume or in the cover letter that accompanies your resume.

Traditionally, an Objective statement is placed in the prominent position just below your contact information. This location helps to focus both the development of your employment record as you write your resume and a recruiter's interpretation of your employment record as they read your resume. In other words, your Objective is the first section of your resume that you write and the first section that an employer will normally read. This focal point acts as a lens through which:

- You evaluate the various details of your work record to determine what to include and what to leave out
- Employers assess your potential fit with their organization and position opening.

⇒⊚ *Helpful Hint*

By including only information that explains and supports your Objective statement in your resume, you create a document with a focused and forceful message that helps employers make accurate judgments of your interests and abilities.

Space on a resume is limited, however, which means that you may have to remove your Objective statement from the document. This section is the only part of your resume where you have an option to save space, and such a move is feasible only because you've used your Objective as the basis for developing all of the other information you've included. Indeed, only remove the statement *after* you complete the final draft of your resume to ensure that every detail included in the document is relevant and appropriate.

If you decide to omit your Objective statement from your resume, you can still communicate this important message to prospective employers. Your cover letter, which should be a companion to every resume you send out to an employer, is an appropriate place to share a description of your employment objective. This letter should relate your background, as described on your resume, to the requirements of the position for which you're applying or the employer's on-going operational needs. To reinforce your message, include your Objective as a key point in your cover letter.

Translating your Objective statement for employers

Your objective in the workplace is different from that of an employer. For example, your Objective may be to obtain a position that would support your ambitions to be the most respected sales representative in your industry. An employer, on the other hand, seeks to fill that position with a sales representative who delivers consistent revenue and profit growth. Similarly, your Objective might be to acquire a position with a higher salary, while the employer wants to recruit a candidate who can get the job done on time and within budget.

As a consequence, your Objective statement must play two very different roles:

- As a statement of what's important to you in the workplace, your Objective's purpose is to focus the development of your resume. The act of creating an Objective statement can help you determine what's relevant and what's immaterial to the presentation of your credentials, which in turn, can tell you what to include—and exclude.
- As a statement of what's important to an employer, your Objective's role is to help sell your qualifications for a specific open position. A well-defined statement can differentiate you from other candidates by underscoring the close fit between your workplace goal and your employer's interests.

Use the original version of your Objective statement to create a tight, coherent portrait of your employment record and capabilities. Send this version to those organizations where you would like to work but have *not* identified a specific opening (in a recruitment ad, Internet job posting or by any other means) for which to apply.

With those organizations where you *have* identified a specific opening for which you are qualified and want to apply, modify your objective to tailor it for that opportunity. Translate your Objective statement from its original expression of your hopes and ambitions to one that addresses the needs of an employer. Whether the statement appears on your resume or in a cover letter, this revision will help you better connect with the prospective employer and sharpen the focus of your record for the specific job you want. Use the following steps to accomplish the translation:

1. Identify the title of the position you seek in an employer's organization. If available, use the exact title provided in the organization's advertisement or job announcement.
2. Pinpoint the benefits you can provide to an organization with your skills and experience. To determine which benefits are of most interest to a specific employer, review the information contained in its recruitment ad or job posting. Look for descriptive terms that indicate a desired quality or outcome, such as "Looking for a fast-starter" or "Seek a manager who can control costs and build revenues." Decide which of the benefits you are most capable of providing.
3. Identify the organization where the open position is located. Be as specific as possible. For example, if you are applying for a position in the Engineering Division of Xerox Corporation, include the division name as well as that of the corporation.
4. Combine the results of Steps 1-3 into a clear and concise Objective statement that expresses your goal in terms relevant to a specific employer. Write out your Objective statement. For example:

OBJECTIVE

A sales representative position in the Xerox Engineering Division where I can apply my technical sales skills and 10 years of industry experience to generate improved revenues at lower costs.

Rewriting your Objective statement for a specific employer has real impact, whether it appears in your resume or in a cover letter. The effort shows an employer that you:

• Have done your homework and identified the employer's needs
• Are serious enough about your application to tailor your Objective to a specific employer
• Understand how to apply your skills and experience to meet the employer's needs.

PINPOINTING THE RIGHT STYLE OF RESUME FOR YOU

When it comes to expressing your credentials, you can choose from several different styles of resumes. As noted in Chapter 1, the three most commonly used styles have both strengths and limitations, and no single resume style can effectively serve the unique circumstances and interests of every person. Therefore, an important key to developing a great resume is the selection of the best style for your particular circumstances.

Understanding the differences

The Table on the following page summarizes the differences between the three main styles of resumes.

In most cases, these differences play out in the Experience section of your resume. They have little or no impact on the placement and content of your Objective, Profile, Education, and Professional Affiliations & Awards sections.

Within the Experience section, the differences clearly affect the kind of information that you include in your resume, how you present that information, and the priority you assign to it. Those factors, in turn, give each resume style unique strengths and limitations with regard to its ability to represent your credentials effectively. These strengths and limitations are summarized in Table 3–2, on page 56.

Selecting the best resume style for you

The characteristics of each resume style and its resulting strengths and limitations make it a more appropriate choice for some individuals than for others. The determining factors are your career path up to the present time and your skill profile. To select the best resume style for you and to learn how to write it, please see Table 3–3. The following definitions will help you interpret the information in the Table.

- Your career path is said to be uninterrupted if you have had no breaks in employment of more than 60 days. An interrupted career path can be caused by such situations as unemployment, a period at home to raise children, an illness, or time spent pursuing an educational degree.

Table 3–1 **Characteristics of Different Resume Styles**	
Name	**Characteristics**
Chronological	Organizes employment information in a historical format, beginning with your most recent job.
	Identifies each position you held by its title, the employer's name and location and the dates you held it.
	Provides a brief description of what you did and your accomplishments in each position.
Functional	Organizes employment information according to your skills and abilities, beginning with your strongest competency.
	Describes your level of expertise in each skill by presenting illustrative situations in which you applied the skill successfully on-the-job.
	Leads with your strength—the capabilities and track record you can bring to an employer.
Hybrid	Includes both a brief chronological summary of your work experience and a description of your functional expertise.
	The chronological summary lists the title of each position you held, the employer's name and location and the dates you worked there.
	The functional description illustrates your level of expertise in selected skills and abilities by presenting situations in which you applied those skills on-the-job.

Table 3–2
Strengths and Limitations of Different Resume Styles

Chronological: Strengths	Limitations
Easy-to-read and understand	Inadequate space to describe skills fully
Emphasizes steady, continuous progression	Spotlights breaks in employment
Recognized and accepted by recruiters and hiring managers	Does not describe nontraditional career paths well
Functional: Strengths	**Limitations**
Highlights what you can do and how well you can do it	Lack of an employment history can make it difficult for recruiters and hiring managers to evaluate you
Enables you to present your qualifications according to your level of expertise	Is difficult to write because you must synthesize your record into skill areas
Effectively describes experience gained via nontraditional career paths	Does not describe organizational advancement well
Hybrid: Strengths	**Limitations**
Combines most strengths of both other styles of resume	Not enough space to detail your work record or qualifications completely
Clear presentation of your employment history	Unusual format may be uncomfortable for some recruiters and hiring managers
Highlights what you can do and how well you can do it	

Table 3–3 Selecting the Appropriate Resume Style			
Career Path To Date	**Skill Profile**	**Resume Style**	**Chapter in This Book**
Uninterrupted	Technical	Hybrid	6
Uninterrupted	General or Managerial	Chronological	4
Interrupted	Technical	Functional	5
Interrupted	General or Managerial	Functional	5

• Your skill profile is technical if your Objective involves the continuous development of your expertise in a particular field of knowledge or profession. Otherwise, your skill profile is general or managerial.

This Table covers everyone in the workforce except first-time job seekers who lack a lengthy work record. If you are looking for your first full-time job, the functional resume is the best style for you. However, its format should be modified to reflect your special strengths. Please see Chapter 7 for more information on how to write a resume for first-time employment.

Chapter 4
Writing a Chronological Resume

A chronological resume presents a history of your employment record, beginning with your most recent position. It identifies the title of each position you held, the organization which employed you, the dates you held the positions, and the tasks you performed.

KNOWING WHEN TO USE A CHRONOLOGICAL RESUME

A chronological resume has several important strengths that make this format a good choice for some job seekers, as well as certain limitations that can degrade its effectiveness for others.

Examining the strengths

As noted in Chapter 3, a chronological resume is usually best if you have a general or managerial background. This style of resume is:

- **Easy-to-read and understand.** Recruiters can quickly determine what you have done in your career, the industries in which you have experience, and the kinds of organizations for which you've worked.
- **A record of continuous progression.** A chronological resume effectively chronicles steady development by presenting your work experience as an unbroken succession of positions with ever-increasing responsibility.
- **Recognized and accepted by recruiters and hiring managers.** The chronological resume is the most prevalent style in the workplace, so recruiters and hiring managers are familiar with its look and comfortable using the information it provides to evaluate candidates.

Exploring the weaknesses

For some job seekers, the chronological resume may not be the best choice of resume style for presenting their qualifications. Relying on a historical perspective,

- **Often does not fully describe your functional capabilities.** Depending on the length of your experience in the workplace, your complete employment history can consume much of the space on a two-page resume and prevent you from presenting all your skills and abilities.
- **Emphasizes breaks in employment.** By providing a historical record of your employment, a chronological resume makes it easy for recruiters to identify interruptions in your career or frequent job changes.
- **Does not effectively describe nontraditional career paths.** Because it is designed to describe your career as a succession of employers and positions with ever-increasing responsibility, a chronological resume is not able to portray alternative career paths effectively—whether they involve periods of unemployment devoted to travel or some other interest or a series of different and unrelated occupational experiences.

✎ *Key Idea*

Based on these factors, a chronological resume will serve you well if your career has involved a steady, continuous series of positions in which you performed increasingly more challenging and important work. This style will probably not work well for you if you're a first-time job seeker with little or no work experience or if your career has followed a nontraditional path.

Knowing where to start—and how to carry through

Regardless of the style you select, preparing a resume can seem like a formidable task at first. By following the seven-step process below, however, you can put together a powerful, persuasive document that will help you to advance your career.

To develop your chronological resume:

1. Collect your employment information. Include any position descriptions and recruitment ads for your previous or current jobs, performance appraisals, project or work descriptions, awards and other professional recognition (such as a certificate of achievement for project contributions), educational record and certificates of completion for training programs, and materials describing your affiliation and participation with professional organizations.
2. Organize your materials into chronological order, beginning with your most recent position and working back to your first job.
3. Prioritize the materials. Use your Objective statement to determine three categories of information:

    * Critical to supporting your Objective and must be included
    * Helpful in supporting your Objective and should be included if space permits
    * Not essential in supporting your Objective and can be omitted

4. Write a first draft of your resume. See the detailed instructions for developing the content and format of your chronological resume in the next section of this chapter.
5. Revise your draft. Modify the information you've presented and, if necessary, delete selected segments in order to keep the length of your document to a maximum of two pages. Only delete information you consider helpful but not critical to supporting your Objective.
6. Edit your draft. Carefully review your document for misspellings and grammatical, typographical, and other errors. Then, ask a friend to review the resume to catch any errors you may have missed and to check that the information you have presented is easy-to-read and understand.
7. Produce your resume. Use a laser or ink jet printer to print out your resume or have the document reproduced at a professional print shop. Use a font size of 11–12 points, high quality white paper, and black ink. Print each page on a separate sheet of paper rather than on the front and back of the same page.

DEVELOPING THE CONTENT OF YOUR CHRONOLOGICAL RESUME

Use the following checklist to develop a great chronological resume. You will build your contact information and Profile, Education, and Professional Affiliations & Awards sections first, and then develop the all important Experience section. If you need additional information about the basic elements of a well-designed resume, please refer to Chapter 2.

Contact information

1. Center your full name at the top of the page and highlight it by using boldface type and a larger font size—such as 14 points—than the size you use in the body of your resume. Include your middle initial, if appropriate, but not your middle name, unless you use it at work.
2. After your name, add the appropriate acronym for any certifications you have received from recognized, independent certifying organizations (for example, CPA for Certified Public Accountant).
3. After your name and any certification, add the appropriate acronym for any doctorate-level degrees you have been awarded by accredited educational institutions (for example, Ph.D. for Doctor of Philosophy), but not degrees at the master's level or below (for example, MA, BA, AA), unless you work in the field of education.
4. Provide your complete mailing address. Position this information one space below your name, on the left-hand side of your resume. Put your street address on one line; the city, state and zip code on the next, as follows:

> 4451 Elm Street
> Andover, MA 02158

5. If possible, provide two methods by which a recruiter or hiring manager can contact you. Position this information one space below your name, on the right-hand side of your resume. Place the preferred method first and the backup method directly below it, as shown below.

> day—(203) 659-2136
> Sam@erols.com

Contact methods include (in order of their effectiveness):

- A private daytime telephone number that you answer
- A private e-mail address that you can check during the day
- A private daytime telephone number that another adult answers
- A nighttime telephone number that you answer
- A private e-mail address that you can check at night

Profile

1. Review your employment materials and identify 3–5 key attributes or qualifications that best support your Objective statement. These capabilities usually are your strongest credentials for the job you seek.
2. Check recruitment ads, job postings on the Internet, and position descriptions, if you have access to them, to determine the terms typically used by employers to express your key credentials.
3. Using the words and phrases favored by employers and recruiters, summarize your qualifications in 3–5 bullets or short phrases.

Education

1. List the education degrees you have earned, using the following format:

   Degree/major, educational institution, location, year awarded

2. List any certificates you have been awarded, using the following format:

   Certificate, certifying organization, year awarded

3. List major training programs you have completed, using the following format:

   Training program, training organization, year completed

4. List any educational course or training program in which you are currently enrolled, citing the course or program, the institution or training organization that is providing it, and the term "Ongoing."

Professional Affiliations & Awards

1. List any license you have earned from a state or other licensing board, using the following format:

License name and number, granting organization, year awarded

2. List any professional societies or associations in which you are a member and/or have held an elected or appointed position. Begin with the term "Member" or the name of the position you held (for example, Program Committee Chair) and then identify the organization by its complete name, and the dates (expressed in years) of your participation (for example 1996–Present).

3. List any awards you have received from professional societies or associations or from your employer, using the following format:

Name or brief description of the award, organization that granted it, year it was presented

4. List any conference presentation you have made, paper you have had published, or program you have helped to organize, using the following format:

Title of the presentation, paper, program or publication, sponsoring organization, date

Experience

List your employers in chronological order beginning with the most recent.

1. State the employer's name and location and your dates of employment on one line, followed by the title of the position you held on the next line. Highlight your position title in bold.

ADEMCo Enterprises   Malden, MA   1991–Present
Project Manager

2. Use action verbs (such as completed, directed, developed, conducted, analyzed) and short, but complete sentences to describe your principal tasks in this position. Limit the information you present to a paragraph of no more than 4–5 lines in length. Focus on activities that support your Objective and illustrate the strengths you highlighted in your Profile. For example:

ADEMCo Enterprises   Malden, MA   1991–Present
Project Manager

Directed six-person team supporting client installation of customer relationship management (CRM) software. Performed site readiness evaluations, coordinated with internal IT Departments, and co-chaired modification review panels. Also oversaw de-bugging routines, client training and follow-on service calls.

3. Identify 2–3 accomplishments that you achieved in this position and highlight them as bullets under the descriptive paragraph. Clearly relate these accomplishments to the activities you described in Step 2. Wherever possible, describe your results using quantitative measures, such as money saved, goods sold, profits earned. For example:

- Accomplished three client installations in two years with no cost overruns or schedule revisions.
- Installed vertical support concept, saving the company over $2 million annually in travel.
- Turned around unhappy client situation, saving a $500,000 sale for the company.

4. Repeat Steps 1–3 above for each position you've held. If you worked in several different positions in the same organization, describe each of the jobs separately, including the dates you held them, but do not repeat the name of the employing organization. For example:

ADEMCo Enterprises   Malden, MA   1991–Present
Project Manager   1997–Present

One paragraph description of your activities
List of 2–3 accomplishments highlighted as bullets

Senior Analyst   1991–1997

One paragraph description of your activities
List of 2–3 accomplishments highlighted as bullets

FORMATTING YOUR CHRONOLOGICAL RESUME

The format of a chronological resume is identical to that of a functional or hybrid resume, except in the Experience section. Organized from most recent to most historically distant, the chronological resume style describes your work experience and credentials through a series of position summaries that detail your previous employers, on-the-job activities, and accomplishments.

Organize the sections of your resume in the following order:

- Contact information
- OBJECTIVE
- PROFILE
- EXPERIENCE
- EDUCATION
- PROFESSIONAL AFFILIATIONS & AWARDS

Except for your contact information, begin each section with its title in all capital letters. As shown in the resume layout in Chapter 2, position the title by itself at the top of the section and aligned with the left hand margin.

⇒◉ *Helpful Hint*

If your resume runs onto a second page, make sure that you include your contact information on that page, as well, just in case one page becomes separated from another. Position this information at the top, left-hand side of the page, as shown below:

Your Name
Your primary contact information
Page Two

The resumes on the following pages illustrate great chronological resumes that put all of these steps together.

Robert P. Weldon

79 East 19th Street   day: (213) 756-8902
Los Angeles, CA 90024   rpw39@aol.com

PROFILE
- Over 15 years experience in production of television broadcasts, film and video
- Winner of 5 Emmys as producer of Public Broadcasting Service travel specials
- Hands-on knowledge of managing projects from conceptualization to airing
- Experience managing production crews, talent and celebrity guests

EXPERIENCE

Public Broadcasting Service   Los Angeles, CA   1989–Present

Senior Producer   1991–Present

Recruited and managed a select team of production professionals creating travel documentaries for public broadcast. Oversaw scripting, casting, logistics and production of three major programs per year, ensuring on-time, on-budget completion. Worked with outside creative talent to design innovative show formats and content, breaking new ground in the production of this genre.

- Successfully produced over 25 programs, generating high audience ratings and earning industry recognition
- Managed a multi-project budget of over $5 million per year for 8 years without a single overrun

Associate Producer   1989–1991

Worked with a production team developing new concepts and themes for public interest programming. Assembled an expert advisory board to review and critique potential initiatives. Designed and implemented several test shows to gauge audience appeal of alternative topics and presentation formats. Analyzed response data and formulated recommendations to senior management.

- Identified core program elements for new action-adventure thrust in public broadcasting
- Established objectives, funding requirements and implementation plans for travel documentaries for children

About Kids   San Diego, CA   1981–1989

Director

Founded this independent film and video production company. Worked with major broadcast and cable television companies nationwide. Produced projects on an array of topics related to child safety, health, development and education. Directed scripting, casting. field production and editing of film programs running from 30 minutes to over 90 minutes in length.

- Built a profitable film company with revenues in excess of $1 million per year
- Produced over 8 shows per year without a single budget overrun
- Show entitled "Kid's Treat" was recognized by the U.S. Department of Education for its innovative presentation of dental care for children

Robert P. Weldon
(213) 756-8902
Page Two

EDUCATION
BA/Communications   Manhattanville College, Purchase, NY   1980

PROFESSIONAL AFFILIATIONS & AWARDS
5 Emmy Awards   National Academy of Television Arts & Sciences   1993–Present
Member   National Academy of Television Arts & Sciences
Member   Directors Guild of America

Jennifer A. Logan

56 Holly Leaf Drive   evening - (703) 897-8921
McLean, VA 22102   jennl@erols.com

PROFILE
- 12-year career of success in sales and marketing
- Experienced in building and managing customer relationships
- Track record of achieving year-to-year increases in revenue and profitability
- Solid background in sales and marketing management software programs and Internet applications

EXPERIENCE

Redmont Mutual Assurance Corporation   Manassas Park, VA   1995–Present
District Sales Manager
Organized new sales territory in northern Virginia. Conceived a plan for sales force recruitment and training, product introduction and business development, distribution channel management and promotion. Sold the plan with supporting budget and corporate support commitments to senior management. Executed the plan to drive growth, outpace the competition and achieve rapid return on investment.
- Beat sales target by 30% in first year of operation
- Won 1998 Leadership Merit Award, Redmont's highest sales and marketing honor
- Expanded sales force to 25 agents in 18 months
- Doubled the territory's new accounts and increased sales per account in second year

Edderton Insurance Group   Charlottesville, VA   1989–1995
Territorial Sales Manager
Focused efforts on recruitment, training and support of independent sales agents marketing insurance products to commercial and large industrial accounts. Concurrently, launched new products and developed field support to enhance revenue performance and bottom-line profitability. Installed new sales lead tracking and management system that improved coordination among agents and responsiveness to customers.
- Won first annual Top of the Heap award for territory leadership
- Built territory to 50+ agents within 3 years
- Appointed to Special Task Force to design "Territory of the Future"

Industrial Insurance Applications Corporation   Charlottesville, VA   1981–1989
Commercial Underwriting Officer
Built 6-person underwriting unit into one of the most productive and efficient operations in the company. Directed daily underwriting operations, long range business planning and all training for newly-hired professional staff. Produced quarterly reports for profit and loss assessment and business management by the Executive Committee and Board of Directors.
- Implemented supplemental educational program for new actuaries that produced passing scores on every actuarial exam taken for three years running
- Created a new software application for actuarial analysis and long-range planning

Jennifer A. Logan
(703) 897-8921
Page Two

Duckettsville Insurance Group   Charlottesville, VA   1979-1981
Field Marketing Representative
Managed field sales and marketing programs throughout central Virginia. Developed new
client leads, established and maintained contact with prospective clients and managed the
start-up of new accounts.
•   Consistently ranked in top 10% of active field agents in the company

EDUCATION
BS/Business Administration   Virginia Tech University, Blacksburg, VA   1979

PROFESSIONAL AFFILIATIONS & AWARDS
Completed 4 qualifying exams   American Actuarial Association   On-going
Member   American Actuarial Association
Member   American Marketing Association

Chapter 5
Writing a Functional Resume

A functional resume presents your primary occupational competencies, beginning with your area of greatest expertise. It describes each of these workplace skills and abilities, illustrates your experience in using them on-the-job, and details the results you achieved.

DECIDING TO USE A FUNCTIONAL RESUME

As noted in Chapter 3, a functional resume is appropriate if you have technical or managerial expertise and your career path has been interrupted (for whatever reason) or you are entering the workforce for the first time. To confirm that it's the best choice for you, carefully evaluate its strengths and limitations.

Assessing the strengths

A functional resume works well if you want to:

- **Highlight what you can do and how well you can do it.** The functional resume helps you to express your potential to a prospective employer by describing how you applied skills and abilities in prior jobs.
- **Present your qualifications according to your level of expertise.** By organizing your employment information based on your performance at work, you can focus on your record of actual achievement rather than on the time you spent in prior positions.
- **Effectively describe a nontraditional career path.** The func-

tional resume concentrates on the skills you have acquired and applied, regardless of the type and sequence of jobs you've held.

Looking at the limitations

To effectively evaluate the functional resume's possible place in your job search efforts, you also need to consider its drawbacks. This style of resume may:

- **Make it difficult for employers to evaluate your work record.** By omitting your employment history, the functional resume forces employers to sift through a less structured presentation of your prior work to gauge the level of experience and track record you bring to a particular job.
- **Be tough to write because you must synthesize your record into skill areas.** Rather than presenting an orderly record of your work history, the functional resume requires that you look across all of your employment experiences to identify and describe your strongest skills and abilities.
- **Obscure organizational advancement.** Because it focuses on your competencies, a functional resume does not provide the framework for demonstrating your steady progress in meeting ever-increasing responsibilities throughout your career history.

K Key Idea

A functional resume will serve you well if you've developed an array of different skills, worked in a variety of unrelated positions, or if you seek to change careers. This style of resume is probably not your best choice if your career has progressed through sustained advancement in a particular company, field or industry.

Knowing where to start—and how to carry through

Regardless of the style you select, preparing a resume can seem like a formidable task at first. By following the seven-step process below, however, you can put together a powerful, persuasive document that will help you to advance your career.

To develop your functional resume:

1. Collect your employment information. Include any position descriptions and recruitment ads for your previous or current jobs, performance appraisals, project or work descriptions, awards and other professional recognition (such as a certificate of achievement for project contributions), educational record and certificates of completion for training programs, and materials describing your affiliation and participation with professional organizations.

2. Organize your materials according to the skills you are/were able to apply on-the-job, beginning with the skill in which you've gained the highest level of expertise.

3. Prioritize the materials. Use your objective statement to determine three categories of information:

   - Critical to supporting your Objective and must be included
   - Helpful in supporting your Objective and should be included if space permits
   - Not essential in supporting your Objective and can be omitted

4. Write a first draft of your resume. See the detailed instructions for developing the content and format of your functional resume in the next section of this chapter.

5. Revise your draft. Modify the information you've presented and, if necessary, delete selected segments in order to keep the length of your document to a maximum of two pages. Only delete information you consider helpful but not critical to supporting your Objective.

6. Edit your draft. Carefully review your document for misspellings and grammatical, typographical, and other errors. Then, ask a friend to review the resume to catch any errors you may have missed and to check that the information you have presented is easy-to-read and understand.

7. Produce your resume. Use a laser or ink jet printer to print out your resume or have the document reproduced at a professional print shop. Use a font size of 11–12 points, high quality white paper, and black ink. Print each page on a separate sheet of paper rather than on the front and back of the same page.

DEVELOPING THE CONTENT OF YOUR FUNCTIONAL RESUME

Use the following checklist to develop a great functional resume. You will build your contact information and Profile, Education and Professional Affiliations & Awards sections first, and then develop the all important Experience section. If you need additional information about the basic elements of a well-designed resume, please refer to Chapter 2.

Contact information

1. Center your full name at the top of the page and highlight it by putting it in boldface type and using a larger font size—such as 14 points—than the size you use in the body of your resume. Include your middle initial, if appropriate, but not your middle name, unless you use it at work.
2. After your name, add the appropriate acronym for any certifications you have received from recognized, independent certifying organizations (for example, CPA for Certified Public Accountant).
3. After your name and any certification, add the appropriate acronym for any doctorate-level degrees you have been awarded by accredited educational institutions (for example, Ph.D. for Doctor of Philosophy), but not degrees at the master's level or below (for example, MA, BA, AA), unless you work in the field of education.
4. Provide your complete mailing address. Position this information one space below your name, on the left-hand side of your resume. Put your street address on one line; the city, state and zip code on the next, as follows:

4451 Elm Street
Andover, MA 02158

5. If possible, provide two methods by which a recruiter or hiring manager can contact you. Position this information one space below your name, on the right-hand side of your resume. Place the preferred method first and the backup method directly below it, as shown below.

day—(203) 659-2136
Sam@erols.com

H *Helpful Hint*

Contact methods include (in order of their effectiveness):

- A private daytime telephone number that you answer
- A private e-mail address that you can check during the day
- A private daytime telephone number that another adult answers
- A nighttime telephone number that you answer
- A private e-mail address that you can check at night

Profile

1. Review your employment materials and identify 3–5 key attributes or qualifications that best support your Objective statement. These capabilities normally are your strongest credentials for the job you seek.
2. Check recruitment ads, job postings on the Internet and position descriptions, if you have access to them, to determine the terms typically used by employers to express your key qualifications.
3. Using the words and phrases favored by employers and recruiters, summarize your qualifications in 3–5 bullets or short phrases.

Education

1. List the education degrees you have earned, using the following format:

   Degree/major, educational institution, location, year awarded

2. List any certificates you have been awarded, using the following format:

   Certificate, certifying organization, year awarded

3. List major training programs you have completed, using the following format:

   Training program, training organization, year completed

4. List any educational course or training program in which you are currently enrolled, citing the course or program, the institution or training organization that is providing it, and the term "Ongoing."

Professional Affiliations & Awards

1. List any license you have earned from a state or other licensing board, using the following format:

   License name and number, granting organization, year awarded

2. List any professional societies or associations in which you are a member and/or have held an elected or appointed position. Begin with the term "Member" or the name of the position you held (for example, Program Committee Chair) and then identify the organization by its complete name and the dates (in years) of your participation (for example, 1996–Present).

3. List any awards you have received from professional societies or associations or from your employer, using the following format:

   Name/brief description of the award, organization that granted it, year it was presented

4. List any conference presentation you have made, paper you've published, or program you have helped to organize, using the following format:

   Title of the presentation, paper, program or publication, sponsoring organization, date

Experience

1. Identify the skill in which you have the greatest level of expertise using a term or phrase that is familiar to employers and recruiters. If you have included the skill in your Profile, repeat the term or phrase you used there. Otherwise, check recruitment ads, job postings on the Internet, and position descriptions, if you have access to them, to determine the term or phrase typically used by employers to express this skill.

2. Describe the skill area by detailing the tasks you performed in various work situations and what outcomes you were able to achieve, as a result. Focus on activities that support your Objective and illustrate the strengths you highlighted in your Profile. Use action verbs and short but complete sentences. If possible, limit the information you

present to a paragraph of no more than 4–5 lines in length. Highlight the name of the skill in bold. For example:

Marketing Program Design & Execution

Pioneered the introduction of conventional marketing concepts into non-traditional markets. Conceptualized, implemented, and managed all aspects of a marketing program to include market research, brand development, service positioning, and client communications. Assessed the performance of several on-going programs and devised enhancements, where necessary.

3. Identify 2–3 of your accomplishments in this skill area. Clearly relate these accomplishments to the activities you describe in the previous step. Wherever possible, describe your results in quantitative measures, such as money saved, goods sold, profits earned. For example:

- Achieved revenue growth of 300% in three years
- Increased brand recognition and stature, yielding 25% increase in new clients
- Earned top 1% rating on annual performance review for two different employers over five years

4. An effective variation of Steps 2–3 is the use of accomplishments as your description of the skill area. In this approach, the information included in each bullet-entry is expanded to detail what you did as well as how well you did it. For example:

- Redirected the marketing strategy of an underperforming product line, achieving revenue growth of 300% in three years.

5. Repeat Steps 1–3/4 above for each of your other skill areas. For best results, be complete, detailed and persuasive in your presentation. Avoid repeating information in the descriptions of your various skills—such as using the same examples or listing the same accomplishments—as doing so may cause employers to view your level of experience as more limited than it really is.

Formatting Your Functional Resume

The format of a functional resume is identical to that of a chronological or hybrid resume, except in the Experience section. In that section, this style describes your work experience and credentials through a series of skill summaries organized by your level of expertise. Each summary details your use of that skill in various positions and the results you achieved.

Organize the sections of your resume in the following order:

*   Contact information
*   OBJECTIVE
*   PROFILE
*   EXPERIENCE
*   EDUCATION
*   PROFESSIONAL AFFILIATIONS & AWARDS

Except for your contact information, begin each section with its title in all capital letters. As shown in the resume layout in Chapter 2, position the title by itself at the top of the section and aligned with the left hand margin.

H   Helpful Hint

If your resume runs onto a second page, make sure that you include your contact information on that page, as well, just in case one page becomes separated from another. Position this information at the top, left-hand side of the page, as shown below:

Your Name
Your primary contact information
Page Two

The resumes on the following pages illustrate great functional resumes that put all of these steps together.

Patrick O'Shay

8724 Deville Avenue
Detroit, MI 48236

day: (313) 982–9802
paddyo@msn.com

PROFILE
- Event Planning and Implementation
- Public Relations and Image Building
- Communications

EXPERIENCE

Event Planning and Implementation

Organized and executed large fund raising projects for both for-profit and not-for-profit organizations. Designed and implemented membership development campaigns. Chaired voluntary programs. Worked with large and small groups to achieve objectives on time and within budget.
- Raised almost $1 million for healthcare program treating at-risk children
- Invigorated volunteer staff of a start-up professional association, leading to increased membership, participation and dues revenue
- Directed United Way program for a large, multi-state corporation, coordinating separate state-based campaigns and increasing pledges by 14%

Public Relations & Image Building

Developed public relations program to attract new members to a new professional association. Coordinated media outreach to enhance public image and stature of the organization. Designed, developed and produced an array of promotional materials, including print, video and computer diskette.
- Increased membership by 16% in the first year and 19% in the following year
- Dramatically expanded brand recognition among key populations, according to focus group testing and surveys
- Increased mentions in the public media by 100%

Communications

Delivered numerous presentations and speeches to a variety of audiences. Appeared on local and national television and radio programs. Chaired meetings and coordinated activities of diverse groups and activities.
- Frequent guest of #1 rated television channel in its market
- Received consistently high marks from audiences at national conventions

EDUCATION
BA/English Literature John Hopkins 1989

PROFESSIONAL AFFILIATIONS & AWARDS
Board of Directors The Put Hope First Foundation
Member American Society of Association Executives

Alan T. Jones

54 Guardian Circle   day: (208) 775-6792
Ithaca, NY 14850   night: (208) 453-8726

OBJECTIVE

An administrative management position with a local municipality where I can deliver improved operating results at reduced costs.

PROFILE

- Twenty-two years of leadership in facilities management.
- Hands-on experience in planning, programming and budgeting for large scale operations.
- Impeccable record in purchasing management, achieving significant savings, reduced waste and improved organizational performance.
- Caring leader who supports the growth and development of subordinates.

EXPERIENCE

Facilities Management

- Consolidated inventory of supplies and equipment, yielding a 17% reduction in storage space requirements and a cost savings of over $50,000 per year.
- Planned, organized and successfully executed a physical relocation of 50 employees and equipment, resulting in minimal disruption to service and genuine improvements in work flow.
- Supervised 10-person staff, providing plumbing, electrical, water and sewer services to a residential community of 350.

Purchasing Management

- Identified requirements for supplies and equipment, solicited vendors and negotiated with selected sources to acquire necessary support on time and within budget.
- Developed procedures to identify and acquire "best value" services and products, reducing customer wait time from five to three days.
- Implemented a follow-up quality assurance program to monitor product/service performance in an installed environment, reducing customer problems and complaints.

Staff Leadership and Development.

- Assessed staff workload, identified unrealistic requirements, obtained new position approvals and recruited and trained new staff to ensure optimum performance and high morale.
- Managed a reorganization that eliminated duplicate positions and reassigned staff into more productive and career-enhancing opportunities.
- Instituted an "open door" policy and resolved personnel issues, helping to reduce attrition by 12%.
- Implemented flexible work schedules to accommodate on-the-job education and employee development of workplace skills and knowledge.

Alan T. Jones
(208) 775-6792
Page Two

EDUCATION
BS/Engineering   North Carolina State University, Raleigh, NC   1987

PROFESSIONAL AFFILIATIONS & AWARDS

Member	Logistics Management Institute
Member	National Society of Professional Engineers (NSPE)
Past President	Ithaca Chapter of NSPE
"Reducing Cycle Time"	A paper presented at the NSPE Annual Conference 1989
Mentor	NSPE Kids in Need Program

NOTES

Chapter 6
Writing a Hybrid Resume

A hybrid resume contains elements of both a chronological and a functional resume. It presents your primary occupational competencies—beginning with your area of greatest expertise—together with a brief history of your employment record—beginning with your most recent position. A hybrid resume:

- Describes your primary workplace skills and abilities
- Illustrates your experience in using these skills on-the-job
- Details the results you achieved
- Identifies the title of each position you held, the organization that employed you, the dates you held the positions, and the tasks you performed.

USING A HYBRID RESUME TO YOUR ADVANTAGE

As noted in Chapter 3, a hybrid resume normally works best if you have enjoyed an uninterrupted career in a technical field. Even if that's the case, however, you should confirm that this format is right for you by evaluating its strengths and limitations.

Evaluating the strengths

A hybrid resume is the right choice if you want a document that

- **Highlights what you can do and how well you can do it.** As with a functional resume, the hybrid style enables you to demonstrate the contribution you can make by describing how you applied specific skills and abilities in your prior jobs.

- **Enables you to present your qualifications according to your level of expertise.** The hybrid resume ensures that you lead with your strength by organizing your employment information based on your primary work capabilities and your performance with those skills.
- **Is easy-to-read and understand.** Because it also includes a brief work history, recruiters can quickly determine what you have done in your career, the industries in which you have had experience, and the kinds of organizations for which you have worked.
- **Emphasizes continuous progression.** As with a chronological resume, the hybrid format also enables you to demonstrate a record of steady development by presenting your work experience as series of positions organized by date.

Sizing up the limitations

When considering whether a hybrid resume might work for you, keep in mind that this style:

- **May not provide an adequate description of either your work record or your qualifications.** By including both chronological and functional information, the hybrid style sometimes lacks the space necessary to describe either your employment history or your functional expertise completely within the desired two-page length of a resume. That limitation can diminish the impact your resume has on recruiters.
- **Can be discomforting for some employers and recruiters.** Because it synthesizes the information contained in both a chronological and a functional resume, the hybrid format doesn't look like most resumes, making it more difficult for employers and recruiters to understand.

K Key Idea

A hybrid resume will serve you well if have a tightly focused set of skills or you want to emphasize your achievements at work more than the positions you've held. You should probably choose a different style if you have progressed through a series of increasingly responsible positions, developed an array of different skills, or worked in a variety of unrelated positions.

Knowing where to start—and how to carry through

Regardless of the style you select, preparing a resume can seem like a formidable task at first. By following the seven-step process below, however, you can put together a powerful, persuasive document that will help you to advance your career.

To develop your hybrid resume:

1. Collect your employment information. Include any position descriptions and recruitment ads for your previous or current jobs, performance appraisals, project or work descriptions, awards and other professional recognition (such as a certificate of achievement for project contributions), educational record and certificates of completion for training programs, and materials describing your affiliation and participation with professional organizations.
2. Organize your materials according to (a) the skills you are/were able to apply on-the-job, beginning with the skill in which you have the highest level of expertise, and (b) your employment chronology, beginning with your most recent position and working back to your first job.
3. Prioritize the materials. Use your Objective statement to determine three categories of information:

    *   Critical to supporting your Objective and must be included
    *   Helpful in supporting your Objective and should be included if space permits
    *   Not essential in supporting your Objective and can be omitted

4. Write a first draft of your resume. See the detailed instructions for developing the content and format of your hybrid resume in the next section of this chapter.
5. Revise your draft. Modify the information you have presented and, if necessary, delete selected segments in order to keep the length of your document to a maximum of two pages. Limit deletions to that information you judge to be helpful but not critical to supporting your Objective.
6. Edit your draft. Carefully review your document for misspellings and

grammatical, typographical, and other errors. Then, ask a friend to review the resume to ensure that you have not overlooked any errors and that the information you have presented is easy-to-read and understand.

7. Produce your resume. Print your resume out with a laser or ink jet printer or have it reproduced at a professional print shop. Use a font size of 11–12 points, high quality white paper, and black ink. Print each page on a separate sheet of paper rather than on the front and back of the same page.

DEVELOPING THE CONTENT OF YOUR HYBRID RESUME

Use the following checklist to develop a great hybrid resume. You will build your contact information and Profile, Education and Professional Affiliations & Awards sections first, and then develop the all important Experience section. If you need additional information about the basic elements in a well-designed resume, please refer to Chapter 2.

Contact information

1. Center your full name at the top of the page and highlight it by using boldface type and a larger font size—such as 14 points—than the size you use in the body of your resume. Include your middle initial, if appropriate, but not your middle name, unless you use it at work.

2. After your name, add the appropriate acronym for any certifications you have received from recognized, independent certifying organizations (for example, CPA for Certified Public Accountant).

3. After your name and any certification, add the appropriate acronym for any doctorate-level degrees you have been awarded by accredited educational institutions (for example, Ph.D. for Doctor of Philosophy), but not degrees at the master's level or below (for example, MA, BA, AA), unless you work in the field of education.

4. Provide your complete mailing address. Position this information one space below your name, on the left-hand side of your resume. Put your street address on one line; the city, state and zip code on the next, as follows:

4451 Elm Street
Andover, MA 02158

5. If possible, provide two methods by which a recruiter or hiring manager can contact you. Position this information one space below your name, on the right-hand side of your resume. Place the preferred method first and the backup method directly below it, as shown below.

day—(203) 659-2136

Sam@erols.com

H *Helpful Hint*

Contact methods include (in order of their effectiveness):

- A private daytime telephone number that you answer
- A private e-mail address that you can check during the day
- A private daytime telephone number that another adult answers
- A nighttime telephone number that you answer
- A private e-mail address that you can check at night

Profile

1. Review your employment materials and identify 3–5 key attributes or qualifications that best support your Objective statement. These capabilities normally are your strongest credentials for the job you seek.

2. Check recruitment ads, job postings on the Internet, and position descriptions, if you have access to them, to determine the terms typically used by employers to express your key credentials.

3. Using the words and phrases favored by employers and recruiters, summarize your qualifications in 3–5 bullets or short phrases.

Education

1. List the education degrees you have earned, using the following format:

Degree/major, educational institution, location, year awarded

2. List any certificates you have been awarded, using the following format:

Certificate, certifying organization, year awarded

3. List major training programs you have completed, using the following format:

Training program, training organization, year completed

4. List any educational course or training program in which you are currently enrolled, citing the course or program, the institution or training organization that is providing it, and the term "Ongoing."

Professional Affiliations & Awards

1. List any license you have earned from a state or other licensing board, using the following format:

License name and number, granting organization, year awarded

2. List any professional societies or associations in which you are a member and/or have held an elected or appointed position. Begin with the term "Member" or the name of the position you held (for example, Program Committee Chair) and then identify the organization by its complete name, and the dates (expressed in years) of your participation (for example 1996–Present).

3. List any awards you have received from professional societies or associations or from your employer, using the following format:

Name or brief description of the award, organization that granted it, year it was presented

4. List any conference presentation you have made, paper you have had published, or program you have helped to organize, using the following format:

Title of the presentation, paper, program or publication, sponsoring organization, date

Experience

1. Identify the skill in which you have the greatest level of expertise, using a term or phrase that is familiar to employers and recruiters. If you have included the skill in your Profile, repeat the term or phrase you used there. Otherwise, check recruitment ads, job postings on the Internet, and position descriptions, if you have access to them, to determine the term or phrase typically used by employers to express this skill.

2. Describe the skill area by detailing the tasks you performed in various work situations and what outcomes you were able to achieve, as a result. Focus on activities that support your objective and illustrate the strengths you highlighted in your profile. Use action verbs and short but complete sentences. If possible, limit the information you present to a paragraph of no more than 4–5 lines in length. Highlight the name of the skill in bold. For example:

Marketing Program Design & Execution

Pioneered the introduction of conventional marketing concepts into non-traditional markets. Conceptualized, implemented, and managed all aspects of a marketing program to include market research, brand development, service positioning, and client communications. Assessed the performance of several on-going programs and devised enhancements, where necessary.

3. Identify 2–3 of your accomplishments in this skill area. Clearly relate these accomplishments to the activities you describe in the previous step. Wherever possible, describe your results in quantitative measures, such as money saved, goods sold, profits earned. For example:

   • Achieved revenue growth of 300% in three years
   • Increased brand recognition and stature, yielding 25% increase in new clients
   • Earned top 1% rating on annual performance review for two different employers over five years

4. Repeat Steps 1–3 above for each of your other skill areas. For best results, be complete, detailed and persuasive in your presentation. Avoid repeating information in the descriptions of your various skills—such as using the same examples or listing the same accomplishments—as doing so may cause employers to view your level of experience as more limited than it really is.

5. Develop a chronology of your employment experience, beginning with your current or most recent position. List the title of each position (in bold), then your employer's name, location and your dates of employment. Place each position with each employer on a separate line. For example:

Project Manager ADEMCo Enterprises Malden, MA 1991–Present

Formatting Your Hybrid Resume

The format of a hybrid resume is identical to that of a chronological or functional resume, except in the Experience section. In the hybrid style, this section describes your work experience and credentials in two separate subsections: a series of skill summaries organized according to your level of expertise followed by a list of your prior positions and employers, in reverse chronological order. As shown below, the employment information is preceded by a title (Employment Chronology) which is centered and underlined.

Organize the sections of your resume in the following order:

- Contact information
- OBJECTIVE
- PROFILE
- EXPERIENCE
                        Employment Chronology
- EDUCATION
- PROFESSIONAL AFFILIATIONS & AWARDS

Except for your contact information, begin each section with its title in all capital letters. As shown in the resume layout in Chapter 2, position the title by itself at the top of the section and aligned with the left hand margin.

H Helpful Hint

If your resume runs onto a second page, make sure that you include your contact information on that page, as well, just in case the pages are separated. Position this information at the top, left-hand side of the page, as shown below:

Your name
Your primary contact information
Page 2

The resumes on the following pages illustrate great hybrid resumes that put all of these steps together.

Jill Ste. Pierre

4534 Jensen Boulevard   day: (202) 554-6979
Washington, DC 20420   jsp@att.worldnet.net

PROFILE
- General Management and Multi-Site Operations
- Recruitment and Training of Staff
- Marketing Communications and Business Presentations

EXPERIENCE

General Management and Multi-Site Operations

Twenty-plus years of experience in budgeting, planning, staffing, marketing and directing multi-site operations, generating $45 million in revenues and consistently high profits. Managed profit and loss (P&L) for fifteen sites in six states. Led team of 11 management personnel and 575 staff. Promoted rapidly throughout career as a result of success in improving bottom-line financial results, strengthening line management and field support teams and achieving performance goals.

- Consistently achieved or surpassed all revenue, profit and margin objectives
- Standardized business reporting and accounting practices, ensuring accurate and timely production of financial information
- Revitalized and enhanced customer service procedures, resulting in 22% gain in repeat business
- Pioneered innovative organizational change initiatives that produced an 18% improvement in on-time performance by service delivery units

Recruitment and Training of Staff

Seasoned business leader who recognizes the importance of recruiting and developing talent for her organization. Oversaw the design and implementation of an aggressive sourcing program to identify and recruit leading candidates for employment. Provided funding and support for in-house employee "university" to deliver high quality, easy access skills training in an array of technical and workplace skills.

- Approved and funded 15-module, 2-week training program, resulting in a 43% increase in certification among nonexempt personnel
- Slashed 85% of external training budget through implementation of in-house, volunteer peer-to-peer training programs

Marketing Communications and Business Presentations

Conceived, wrote, produced and delivered hundreds of presentations to executives, line managers and field staff. Led effort to reformulate brand and reposition the company in the marketplace. Built entire public communications strategy for new brand introduction. Designed and oversaw production of consumer-based marketing promotions and ad campaigns.

- Successfully established a new brand identity for the company
- Focus group testing indicated a new and higher level of awareness for the company's products and services

Jill Ste. Pierre
(202) 554-6979
Page Two

<u>Employment Chronology</u>
Management Consultant   Self-employed, McLean, VA   1995–Present
Director/Division Manager   Motel 1 Group, Washington, DC   1988–1995
Business Manager   Marriott International, Rockville, MD   1978–1988
Marketing Manager   Jefferson Commercial Real Estate, Arlington, VA   1975–1978

EDUCATION

BA/Speech & Communications   University of Virginia, Charlottesville, VA   1975

Executive Development Program   Darden School of Business, University of Virginia, Charlottesville, VA, 1985

MBA/Marketing   American University, Washington, DC   On-going

PROFESSIONAL AFFILIATIONS & AWARDS

Member   American Management Association

James X. Stoffard

1775 Alicia Court
Wilmington, NC 28207

day: (704) 843-5746
james249@aol.com

OBJECTIVE
A Vice President of Business Development position where I can implement innovative programs to generate rapid revenue and profit growth for an industry leader.

PROFILE
- Market Research
- Revenue and Profit Growth
- Marketing Campaign Management
- Competitive Analysis
- Customer Relationship Management

EXPERIENCE

Market Research
Founded market research organization and built the business to #2 in the region within six years. Pioneered the use of online marketing strategies for an array of commercial products and services. Developed complete marketing programs to include market research, product/service positioning, incentive sales programs, client communications strategies and brand development initiatives.
- Developed profitable new markets for mature products and services
- Increased customer retention and solidified market position by incorporating distinctive value-added components in product sales proposition
- Built a company into a regional leader within a highly competitive market

Revenue Growth and Business Development
Developed management team and corporate culture necessary to accelerate revenue growth in an under-performing service business. Built sales team and established incentive program to achieve rapid return to profitability. Negotiated key partnerships and alliances.
- Increased revenue by 200% in just four years
- Expanded market penetration by creating distinctive selling propositions
- Grew repeat sales by using technological innovation to enhance client satisfaction

Marketing Campaign Management
Employed proven marketing strategies and techniques to create numerous marketing campaigns. Performed market research, competitive analysis, surveys and personal selling in a sensitive and highly visible public position. Worked with radio, television and print media to craft highly focused and compelling messages.
- Pioneer in the use of database marketing strategies and targeted direct mail campaigns
- Demonstrated excellence in public speaking and media appearances
- Oversaw ad agency that was nominated for a national industry award

James X. Stoffard
(704) 843-5746
Page Two

Competitive Analysis
Conducted market research for a number of clients to identify their current and prospective competitors. Acquired public and private information on the competitors' strengths and weaknesses and, to the extent possible, on their plans for new product introductions that could adversely affect the client. Evaluated the threat posed by each competitor and identified positioning strategies and marketing themes to counter them.
- Analyses helped clients successfully launch major new products and strengthen the position of those already in the marketplace.
- Received a letter of commendation from a client CEO, expressing his gratitude for the insights and opportunities identified by the analyses.

Relationship Management and Client Retention
Established relationship management culture and infrastructure for sales organization. Taught and modeled the concept of a "relationship for life," to help sales agents appreciate the importance of long term client relationships and accept responsibility for them. Created programs to reward both sales agents and customers for sustaining relationships.
- Consistently generated revenues at six times the industry average per client
- Awarded corporate Superior Achievement Commendation
- Reduced cost of new client acquisition by 15%

Employment Chronology
President/COO Piedmont Marketing Services, Wilmington, NC 1992–Present
Vice President/Marketing Beltone Mobile Systems of North Carolina,
   Wilmington, NC 1977–1992
Marketing Manager Communications Maintenance Associates, Carmel, CA
   1972–1977

EDUCATION
MBA   University of North Carolina, Chapel Hill, NC   1992
BA/Art History   Indiana University, Bloomington, IN   1972

PROFESSIONAL AFFILIATIONS & AWARDS
Participant   Leadership Carolina
Member   American Marketing Association

Chapter 7
Writing a Great Resume
If You're Looking for Your First Job

IN THIS CHAPTER

- Figuring out what counts on your resume
- Creating a resume with all the right stuff
- Organizing your stuff for maximum impact

First-time job seekers are best served by a modified functional resume. This format presents your primary employment capabilities, beginning with your area of greatest expertise. The resume describes each of your workplace skills and abilities and illustrates your experience in using them in both paid employment and in other, unpaid activities.

GATHERING EVIDENCE OF YOUR CAPABILITIES

Creating an effective resume begins as a research project. You want to identify and collect all of the information that describes the skills and knowledge you've acquired—in school, extracurricular and other non-work activities and on-the-job—and any experience you've had in the workplace.

Looking beyond paid employment

If you're a first-time job seeker, your formal employment experience is probably limited to part-time jobs and full-time positions during summer breaks from school. These situations are important because they enable you to demonstrate your skills in a paid work environment. You also can demonstrate your employability by describing your unpaid work in other areas, including internships, school activities, volunteer contributions, and even your hobbies and other interests. The following definitions can help you focus on those situations worthy of a mention in your resume:

- **Internships** include any workplace function or activity performed under the guidance or sponsorship of an academic institution, employer, or other organization.
- **School activities** include any extracurricular programs in which you participated as a student, including student government, clubs, issue advocacy, and athletics.
- **Volunteer work** includes any role you had in civic, social, community, or other programs designed to assist, support, or promote specific organizations or causes.

⚑ *Red Flag*

We live in an imperfect world, and some employers may not appreciate some of the causes and issues for which you have worked. Therefore, play it safe and cite only those that are not controversial or antagonistic to the business community.

- **Hobbies and interests** include any groups in which you participated that were organized by those with similar interests or passions.

Recognizing your accomplishments

Unpaid work activities enable recruiters and employers to identify your skills and abilities even when you haven't been paid directly for using your time, energy, and talents. Your accomplishments help in the assessment of your level of expertise in those skills and abilities. Accomplishments can include any awards or recognition you received or results you achieved through your participation.

Knowing where to start—and how to carry through

Preparing a resume can seem like a formidable task at first. By following the seven-step process below, however, you can put together a powerful, persuasive document that will help you successfully launch your career.
    To develop your resume:

1. Collect your employment information. Include any position descriptions and announcements for your previous or current paid and unpaid work, project or work descriptions, academic and work-related awards and recognition, educational record, and materials

describing your affiliation and participation with the student chapters of professional organizations.

2. Organize your materials according to the skills you are/were able to apply in these activities, beginning with the skill in which you have developed the highest level of expertise.

3. Prioritize the materials. Use your Objective statement to determine three categories of information:

    - Critical to supporting your Objective and must be included
    - Helpful in supporting your Objective and should be included if space permits
    - Not essential in supporting your Objective and can be omitted

4. Write a first draft of your resume. See the next section for detailed instructions on developing the content and format of your resume.

5. Revise your draft. Modify the information you've presented and, if necessary, delete selected segments in order to keep the length of your document to a maximum of two pages. Limit deletions to that information you judge to be helpful but not critical to supporting your Objective.

6. Edit your draft. Carefully review your document for misspellings and grammatical, typographical, and other errors. Then, ask a friend to review the dresume to ensure that you didn't miss any errors and that the information you have presented is easy-to-read and understand.

7. Produce your resume. Print your resume out with a laser or ink jet printer or have it reproduced at a professional print shop. Use a font size of 11–12 points, high quality white paper, and black ink. Print each page on a separate sheet of paper rather than on the front and back of the same page.

DEVELOPING YOUR RESUME'S CONTENT

The following checklist provides a framework for building a great resume that presents a solid account of your credentials and job-related goals. You will build your contact information and Profile, Education and Professional Affiliations & Awards sections first, and then develop the all important Experience section. If you need additional information about the basic elements of a well-designed resume, refer to Chapter 2.

Contact information

1. Center your full name at the top of the page and highlight it by putting it in boldface type and using a larger font size—such as 14 points—than the size you use in the body of your resume. Include your middle initial, if appropriate, but not your middle name, unless you use it at work.

2. After your name, add the appropriate acronym for any certifications you have received from recognized, independent certifying organizations (for example, CPA for Certified Public Accountant).

3. After your name and any certification, add the appropriate acronym for any doctorate-level degrees you have been awarded by accredited educational institutions (for example, Ph.D. for Doctor of Philosophy), but not degrees at the master's level or below (for example, MA, BA, AA), unless you work in the field of education.

4. Provide your complete mailing address. Position this information one space below your name, on the left-hand side of your resume. Put your street address on one line; the city, state and zip code on the next, as follows:

4451 Elm Street
Andover, MA 02158

5. If possible, provide two methods by which a recruiter or hiring manager can contact you. Position this information one space below your name, on the right-hand side of your resume. Place the preferred method first and the backup method directly below it, as shown below.

day—(203) 659-2136
Sam@erols.com

H   Helpful Hint

Contact methods include (in order of their effectiveness):

- A private daytime telephone number that you answer
- A private e-mail address that you can check during the day
- A private daytime telephone number that another adult answers
- A nighttime telephone number that you answer
- A private e-mail address that you can check at night

Profile

1. Review your employment materials and identify 3–5 key attributes or qualifications that best support your Objective statement. These capabilities normally are your strongest credentials for the job you seek.
2. Check recruitment ads, job postings on the Internet and position descriptions, if you have access to them, to determine the terms typically used by employers to express your key qualifications.
3. Using the words and phrases favored by employers and recruiters, summarize your qualifications in 3–5 bullets or short phrases.

Education

1. List the education degrees you have earned or will earn upon graduation, using the following format:

   Degree/major, educational institution, location, year awarded

2. On the line directly below your education degree, list any academic awards or scholarships you received and your grade point average, if it's is equal to a B (3.3 on a 4.0-pint scale) or higher. Use the following format:

   Degree/major, educational institution, location, year awarded
   Grade Point Average 3.67/4.00
   Tau Epsilon Engineering Honor Society

3. List any certificates you have been awarded, using the following format:

   Certificate, certifying organization, year awarded

Professional Affiliations & Awards

1. List any professional societies or associations in which you are/were a student member. Begin with the term "Student Member" and then identify the organization by its complete name and list the year(s) you participated.
2. List the student chapter or affiliate of any professional societies or associations in which you have held an elected or appointed position. Begin with the title of the position you held and then identify

the organization by its complete name and list the year(s) you held the position.

3. List any awards you have received from professional societies or associations, using the following format:

Name/brief description of the award, organization which granted it, year it was presented.

4. List any conference presentation you have made, paper you have had published or program you helped to organize, using the following format:

Title of the presentation, paper, program or publication, sponsoring organization, date

Experience

1. Identify the skill in which you have the greatest level of expertise, using a term or phrase that is familiar to employers and recruiters. If you have included the skill in your Profile, repeat the term or phrase you used there. Otherwise, check recruitment ads, job postings on the Internet and position descriptions, if you have access to them, to determine the term or phrase typically used by employers to express this skill.

2. Describe the skill area by detailing the tasks you performed in various work situations (unpaid as well as paid) and what outcomes you were able to achieve. Focus on activities that support your Objective and illustrate the strengths you highlighted in your Profile. Use action verbs and short but complete sentences. If possible, limit the information you present to a paragraph of of 4–5 lines in length. Put the name of the skill in bold. For example:

Project Management

Chaired a task force for the Student Government Association to identify alternative financing options for on-campus entertainment events. Surveyed leading colleges and universities around the country to determine their methods. Interviewed university's Vice President of Finance to get his perspective. Developed a slate of options and presented them to the Association's Executive Committee for decision.

3. Identify 2–3 of your accomplishments in this skill area. Clearly relate these accomplishments to the activities you described in Step 2.

Wherever possible, describe them using quantitative measures, such as money saved, goods sold, profits earned. For example:

- Completed project two months prior to assigned deadline
- Selected option increased revenues from student programs by 15% in six months
- Personal leadership of the project was recognized in a letter of appreciation from Student Government Association president

4. Alternatively, if you have limited or no work experience, describe each of your skill areas with a list of bullets detailing the specific knowledge and/or capabilities you have acquired through your education. This list should not restate the syllabus for your course work, but instead, identify only those areas where you have achieved genuine mastery.
5. Repeat Steps 1–3/4 above for each of your other skill areas. For best results, be complete, detailed and persuasive in your presentation. Avoid repeating information in the descriptions of your various skills—such as using the same examples or listing the same accomplishments—as doing so may cause employers to view your level of experience as more limited than it really is.

Formatting Your Resume

A modified version of a standard functional resume is the best format for first-time job seekers. The modification occurs in the placement of your Experience section. In that section, the resume describes your work experience and credentials through a series of skill summaries that are organized by your level of expertise. Each summary details your use of that skill in various positions and the results you achieved.

Because you've spent less time in the workplace than those with more experience, your resume leads with your strength. This strength is the exposure your recent education has given you to the latest concepts and knowledge in your field. Therefore, you should position your Education section before that of your Experience section in order to highlight this aspect of your qualifications.

To summarize, the information in your resume will be organized as follows:

- Contact information
- OBJECTIVE

- PROFILE
- EDUCATION
- EXPERIENCE
- PROFESSIONAL AFFILIATIONS & AWARDS

Except for your contact information, begin each section with its title in all capital letters. As shown in the resume layout in Chapter 2, position the title by itself at the top of the section and aligned with the left hand margin.

H *Helpful Hint*

If your resume runs onto a second page, make sure that you include your contact information on that page, as well, just in case one page becomes separated from another. Position this information at the top, left-hand side of the page, as shown below:

Your name
Your primary contact information
Page 2

The resumes on the following pages illustrate great functional resumes that are tailored for a first-time job seeker.

Richard Johnson

1819 Altine Avenue, Apartment 3C
Westlake Village, CA 91362

day: (805) 891–7690
pager: (888) 555–2682

PROFILE
• Management and Supervision
• Financial Administration
• Data Systems Operation

EDUCATION
BA/Business Administration California State University, Long Beach, CA
Expected June, 2006

EXPERIENCE
Management and Supervision
While still a full-time student, supervised a grocer's night shift of 12 employees. Directed operations involving logistics, maintenance, inventory control and quality assurance. Trained new employees.
• One of this retail grocery chain's youngest supervisors
• Earned superior ratings from Store Manager
• Worked effectively with people of all ethnic backgrounds and ages

Financial Administration
Performed accounts payable function for University library. Logged all correspondence. Scheduled invoices for payment. Answered inquiries from vendors and supported Comptroller with special projects.
• Improved filing system and reduced errors in accounts payable administration
• Given increased responsibilities based on superior performance
• Gained in-depth knowledge of financial management software programs

Data Systems Operation
Selected for student financial aid position in University Computer Operations Department. Quickly learned all data entry procedures and performed assigned tasks with a minimum of supervision. Learned PC applications, including Windows Excel and Access.
• Recognized by the Department Manager for on-time, error-free performance

PROFESSIONAL AFFILIATIONS & AWARDS
Member Student Chapter, American Institute of Certified Public Accountants (AICPA)
Member Student Investing Club

Clifford R. Early

Tufts University   day: (617) 838–9825
15 Ophelia Hall, Medford, MA 02121   cliffe@tufts.edu

OBJECTIVE
A systems engineering position with a cutting edge company where I can apply my education to help create state-of-the-art products.

PROFILE
- Applications oriented
- Schooled and practiced in experimental and analytical methods
- Demonstrated ability to collaborate with and lead project teams
- Modeling, control and integration of dissimilar technologies

EDUCATION
MS/Computer & Systems Engineering Tufts University, Medford, MA
   Expected May 2006
Grade Point Average of 4.0/4.0

BS/Electrical Engineering Rochester Polytechnic Institute, Troy, NY   1997
Cum laude

EXPERIENCE
Control System Design & Analysis
- Classical control, notably root-locus and bode design methods
- Multiple input, multiple output state space analysis
- System identification techniques applied to bulk forming
- Path planning optimization for manufacturing processes

System Modeling
- Frequency and time domain, input-output and state space, nonlinear methods, Monte-Carlo and probabilistic analyses, computational and analytic model development
- Deformation modeling based on upper-bound analysis and thermal modeling for real-time control applications
- Electro-hydraulic and direct-drive valves, hydraulic motors and rams
- Lasers, detectors, molecular filters, scattering and performance, power and noise modeling for velocity sensing

System Design and Testing
- Architecture design and development
- Hardware and software partitioning issues
- System performance testing
- Failure detection, isolation and correction
- System self-test development

Clifford R. Early
(617) 838-9825
Page Two

Electronic and Instrumentation Design
- Analog electronics design
- Servo loops
- High frequency amplifiers
- Data acquisition system development
- Extrusion press sensor integration
- State machines
- Programmable logic devices
- Computer interfaces

Leadership
- Participated on and led project teams
- Defined and planned new projects
- Taught and mentored undergraduate students

PROFESSIONAL AFFILIATIONS & AWARDS

Member   Tau Beta Pi Engineering Honor Society

Member   IEEE and its Control Systems Special Interest Group

"Application of Modeling Techniques to Structural Integrity Problems"
with Andus Freinze, a paper presented at 7th IEEE Conference on
Control Applications 1998

NOTES

Chapter 8
Writing an Electronic Resume

IN THIS CHAPTER

- Understanding the new technology found in today's Human Resource Departments
- Creating a version of your resume that will work effectively with this technology
- Putting this state-of-the-art resume onto paper

Today, a great resume is one that describes your employment credentials with clarity and power *and* presents that information in a way that's compatible with the advanced technology now being used by many Human Resource Departments.

UNDERSTANDING THE STATE-OF-THE-ART HR DEPARTMENT

A quiet but pervasive technological revolution has occurred in the Human Resource Departments of both large and small employers in the United States.

Recognizing the role of scanners and computers

In the past, Human Resource Departments largely worked with paper. They used paper resumes to evaluate candidates for their current openings and paper files to store those resumes for consideration when other jobs opened in the future. This process worked because the pace of recruiting was relatively relaxed, and the number of candidates involved was small.

Today, however, employers face a very different environment:

- Job openings occur much more frequently and in much larger numbers as organizations continually shift their product and service strategies, facility locations, and markets.
- The number of candidates has increased dramatically as more indi-

viduals assume responsibility for managing their own careers. In addition, staff reductions have thrown many individuals who would not normally be looking for a new job into the job market.

- In order to reduce overhead costs, many companies have downsized their Human Resource staffs.
- Senior managers and executives are more aware of the serious impact that unfilled positions can have on an organization's operations and its bottom line.

The net result of these factors has been a fundamental change in the way many HR Departments handle resumes. Today, most organizations use computer-based resume management systems to accept, process, store, and review these documents.

Computer-based resume management systems typically have three components:

- **A scanner.** This device uses optical character recognition technology to take a picture of your resume and translate it into information that computers can accept and use.
- **A computerized database.** This area of the system stores the information contained on resumes so that it can be quickly retrieved for review when needed.
- **A search engine.** This software application enables recruiters to locate specific resumes in the database that match the requirements for their open positions.

Typically, a resume management system is used in an administrative process, as described below:

1. Resumes are received in the HR Department, removed from their envelopes and quickly evaluated to determine if they can be scanned.

⚑ *Red Flag*

Those resumes that cannot be scanned are usually discarded, often without telling the individuals who sent them.

2. Acceptable resumes are scanned and then input into the computer's database. Unfortunately, HR Departments often don't have the staff to

review the accuracy of the scanner's copy or to correct any errors it may make.
3. The scanned document is then available for search by recruiters who are seeking candidates for open positions. Recruiters specify "keywords" to the search engine, which then reads every word in every resume to identify those documents that contain matching words.
4. The information the selected resumes contain is further reviewed, and a decision is made about each individual's qualifications for specific open positions. Potentially qualified candidates begin assessment and interviewing, while the resume records of those judged not qualified are returned to the database.

Braving the new world of scanners

Every step of the HR screening process contains obstacles for your resume. If you carefully consider these points, your resume has a better chance of making it through the initial stages of processing:

- If you send your resume to an employer that is not in a suitable format for scanning, the employer may discard it and you will not be considered for the opportunities available at that employer.
- If your resume makes it through the scanning process, but contains formatting and other word processing conventions that are not compatible with the scanner, the resulting computer file may contain numerous errors that will not be detected before it is input into the computer's database.
- Finally, if the electronic file containing your resume has numerous errors or terms that do not match the keywords that the recruiters use, the search engine will not find and match your resume to their open positions.

⚙ *Key Idea*

You may have written a great resume, but if the document is not compatible with the technology in today's HR Department, you may be overlooked, even if you are qualified for a particular position.

While resume management systems are not found in every HR Department, they are used by virtually every large employer and, increasingly, by small to mid-sized organizations, as well. Moreover, you're not likely to know which HR Departments do and which do not use this technology. Therefore, the safest course is to *assume that every employer is using it and prepare accordingly.*

What does this assumption mean for your resume? Unless you know for sure that an employer is still relying on a paper-based process for keeping track of resumes, you need to reconfigure your document into an electronic resume—one that is computer-friendly.

WRITING A COMPUTER-FRIENDLY VERSION OF YOUR RESUME

To transform your resume into a document that is acceptable to computers, you have to adjust both its format and its content. However, the resulting electronic resume can and should be appealing for the human recruiter, as well, so that you can use it for all of your job searching and career management requirements.

Adapting your resume to a universal electronic format

Scanners are fickle machines. They are generally reliable when information is presented in a form that they can easily recognize, but are highly unreliable when information appears in other styles or formats. For example, if you emphasize the word engineer in your resume by underlining it, most scanners will not be able to read the letters accurately. As a result, the word may be translated into such gibberish as *etttjurrneeet* by the computer, essentially guaranteeing that a keyword search will be unable to match you for an engineer position.

To ensure that a scanner will read the information on your resume correctly, adhere to the following Do's and Don'ts in formatting your resume:

* ***Do*** use a font size of 11–12 points. The text will be large enough for the scanner to read, but won't use too much space on your resume.
* ***Do*** use a typeface that is simple and clean, such as Arial, Tahoma or Verdana.
* ***Do*** use bold lettering in moderation. Limit bolding to key information that you want to emphasize (such as the titles of positions you've held)
* ***Do*** use bullets, but ensure that they are solid bullets (•). Scanners may read open bullets as the letter "o".

- **Do not** use underlining or italics.
- **Do not** use columns or other landscaping techniques. Scanners read from left to right and often distinguish each column as a separate page of information.
- **Do not** use shading. In order to read a word accurately, scanners need as much contrast as possible between the letters in the word and the background of the page.
- **Do not** use boxes or other graphics. Scanners often read the vertical line in a box as an "I" and thus completely misread the information it contains.

These guidelines can help to ensure that your resume's information is accurately scanned and input into the database of a computer-based resume management system. That's a critical first step because the information that gets put into the database determines whether your resume is ever identified for the kind of job you want.

Reworking your resume's content

Computers locate specific resumes stored in their databases by matching the words contained in each resume with keywords that the recruiter specifies. These keywords normally are nouns and phrases that describe the credentials a person must have to be considered qualified for an open position.

Computers cannot read between the lines or draw inferences from other information that your resume contains. Computers can only make comparisons and identify exact matches. For example, if a recruiter uses the keywords "human resources management" as the search criteria, the computer will find any resume with that precise wording, but not any resume in which:

- A term varies even slightly (such as human resource management)
- A synonym is used (such as "personnel administration"), even though both terms often are essentially interchangeable
- Any word is misspelled (such as "human resources managfement").

H Helpful Hint
_____

The key to creating an effective electronic resume is to ensure that you include *all* of the possible keywords that recruiters may use to identify a candidate with your qualifications and experience. You also need to be sure that you spell every word on your resume correctly.

How do you determine what keywords recruiters are likely to use? Check out these resources:

* Recruitment ads in newspapers and other publications
* Job postings at employment-related sites on the Internet
* Position descriptions or other documents used by HR Departments to detail a job's functions and skills requirements
* Recruiters and Human Resource professionals you may know or whom you can contact.

Identify the most common nouns and phrases HR Departments use to describe a candidate who is qualified for a job similar to the one you want. Then, use *their* vocabulary to describe your applicable skills, knowledge, and experience. As noted in Chapters 2 and 3, these terms should appear, as appropriate, in every section of your resume, including your Objective and Profile.

For example, the following job posting is rich in keywords.

Vice President
Manufacturing

Exceptional leadership opportunity for results-focused manufacturing professional to take full P&L responsibility for our multi-plant, mid-south operations. Your experience base should include general management, turnaround, and a record of success in achieving business growth and profit. Career history should reflect progressive management assignments. A solid background in high-volume metalworking and assembly in a large plant environment essential. Extensive knowledge of manufacturing processes, materials, automation, and cell manufacturing a prerequisite. Skill base should include capital planning, budget and cost controls, labor management, and overhead and inventory optimization. Exposure to cast processing a plus. Management style should be take-charge, team-centered, and foster accountability. Bachelor's degree and continuing education required.

The keywords include:

- P&L responsibility (i.e., profit & loss responsibility)
- Multi-plant operations
- Turnaround experience
- High volume metal working and assembly
- Large plant environment
- Manufacturing processes, materials, automation
- Cell manufacturing
- Capital Planning
- Budget and cost controls
- Overhead and inventory optimization
- Labor management
- Cast processing
- Bachelor's degree
- Continuing education

If these terms describe qualifications similar to your own, they would be appropriate keywords to include in your resume.

PRODUCING YOUR COMPUTER-FRIENDLY RESUME

The final production of your resume as well as the way you deliver the document to employers can affect how a computer responds to this very important record. Factors such as ink and paper color and paper quality also can have an impact on how well your resume scans.

Selecting paper and ink for your electronic resume

Scanners work best when the words in your resume are in sharp color contrast to the paper on which they are printed. Therefore, avoid using cream or buff colored paper—although both are often recommended by traditional resume guides—because those colors can diminish the level of contrast between the print and the page. In addition, do not use blue, brown, or other eye-catching ink colors. Instead, stick with black ink and a high grade of bright white paper. The combination may have less visual impact for humans, but scanners love it.

Make sure that you use a laser or ink jet printer and a fresh ink cartridge to print your resume. Do not use a dot-matrix printer, as many scanners can't read the copies printed with these machines. If you do not have access to a high-grade printer, use a commercial print shop to reproduce your resume.

The right grade of paper is also important. Although formerly fashionable, resumes reproduced on parchment or other heavy grades of paper often cause scanners to choke. To get the best results, use copier (20 lb.) or offset printing (60 lb.) paper. In addition, always use the standard paper size of 8.5-x-11 inches.

▶ *Red Flag*

If your resume runs more than one page in length, use two separate sheets of paper rather than using both sides of the same page. Otherwise, the scanner has to be stopped, your resume retrieved, turned over and run again in order to get all of the information into the system. That means extra work for the scanner operator, assuming that he or she even notices that your resume is printed on the front and back. The worst consequence, of course, is that only half of your resume is successfully scanned and entered in the database.

Sending your electronic resume to employers

While poor formatting and content create many of the problems associated with processing resumes through a resume management system, the way you send your resume to an employer can also undermine its effectiveness. Therefore, use the following guidelines when forwarding your document to an HR Department:

- Always send your resume *unfolded* in a large envelope. The creases created when you fold a resume for a normal #10 business envelope can mar the clarity of the printed text.
- Always *paperclip* the pages of your resume together. The HR Department will separate all pages for scanning, and removing staples can damage your resume and affect its processing.

Transforming your resume into a computer-friendly layout enhances your effectiveness in the job market. The following document shows how you can highlight your employment credentials and enable an employer to input your qualifications accurately into a resume management system.

Your Name

Your street address   Telephone #
Your city, town, zip   E-mail address

OBJECTIVE
Use keywords wherever possible to describe your employment Objective and relate it to an employer's requirements and mission.

PROFILE
Use keywords to detail your primary skills, knowledge, abilities, and experience.

EXPERIENCE
Your position title or key skill area
Use skill words and their synonyms in a 4-5 line paragraph that describes what you did in this position or how you demonstrated this skill area at work.
• List 1-3 accomplishments, setting each off with a solid bullet.

Your position title or key skill area
Use skill words and their synonyms in a 4-5 line paragraph that describes what you did in this position or how you demonstrated this skill area at work.
• List 1-3 accomplishments, setting each off with a solid bullet.

Your position title or key skill area
Use skill words and their synonyms in a 4-5 line paragraph that describes what you did in this position or how you demonstrated this skill area at work.
• List 1-3 accomplishments, setting each off with a solid bullet.

Your position title or key skill area
Use skill words and their synonyms in a 4-5 line paragraph that describes what you did in this position or how you demonstrated this skill area at work.
• List 1-3 accomplishments, setting each off with a solid bullet.

Your position title or key skill area
Use skill words and their synonyms in a 4-5 line paragraph that describes what you did in this position or how you demonstrated this skill area at work.
• List 1-3 accomplishments, setting each off with a solid bullet.

Your position title or key skill area
Use skill words and their synonyms in a 4-5 line paragraph that describes what you did in this position or how you demonstrated this skill area at work.
• List 1-3 accomplishments, setting each off with a solid bullet.

EDUCATION
List your degrees using the terms most prevalent among recruiters. If space permits, use both the complete name and its acronym—Master of Business Administration (MBA).

PROFESSIONAL AFFILIATIONS & AWARDS
List your professional activities and awards, using keywords, wherever appropriate.

NOTES

Chapter 9
Developing an Internet Resume

IN THIS CHAPTER

- Using the Internet to find a new or better job
- Creating a version of your resume for use online
- Sending your resume over the Internet

According to recent surveys, almost ninety percent of all employers and a growing number of staffing firms, employment agencies, and executive recruiters are now using the Internet to identify candidates for open positions. In order to take advantage of these opportunities, however, you must tailor your resume for use on the Internet and know where and how to send it online.

UNDERSTANDING HOW EMPLOYERS AND RECRUITERS USE THE INTERNET

Employers and third-party recruiters—staffing firms and employment agencies—are always seeking quicker, less expensive methods of finding high-quality candidates for their open positions. Traditionally, they have had to rely on relatively expensive print advertisements and time-consuming networking to make these connections. With the advent of the Internet, however, employers and third-party recruiters have a versatile medium that offers them considerable cost and time advantages.

The number of employment-related sites on the Internet and World Wide Web has increased dramatically since the early 1990s. Today, more than 40,000 of these destinations exist, operated by commercial recruitment companies, professional and trade associations, government agencies, and employers themselves. Table 9–1 on the following page lists some of the more popular sites, based on their visitor traffic and focus.

Employers use these sites for two purposes: posting announcements of open positions and searching for resumes stored in databases maintained by the sites.

Table 9–1
Employment Related Web-Sites

Site Name	Site's Internet Address/URL
America's Job Bank	www.ajb.dni.us
Best Jobs USA	www.bestjobsusa.com
Career Builder Network	www.careerbuilder.com
CareerJournal.com	www.careerjournal.com
CoolWorks.com	www.coolworks.com
DICE	www.dice.com
ExecuNet	www.execunet.com
FlipDog.com	www.flipdog.com
Medzilla	www.medzilla.com
Monster.com	www.monster.com
Net-Temps.com	www.net-temps.com
Science Careers	www.sciencecareers.org
USAJOBS	www.usajobs.gov
VetJobs.com	www.vetjobs.com
Yahoo! HotJobs	www.hotjobs.com

Checking out online job postings

A job posting is the electronic equivalent of a classified ad. It describes the skills, knowledge, and experience an employer requires for an open position and identifies one or more methods by which you can submit your resume for consideration. In addition, the posting may also provide information about the employer.

A site may have as few as five or six job postings and as many as several hundred thousand. In most cases and particularly at the larger sites, these openings are stored in a computerized database. They are invisible until you tell the computer the specific kind of job in which you're interested.

The computer's search engine looks through all of the openings stored in its database and lists those that match your criteria.

A job posting isn't especially eye-appealing, but does provide useful information. Here's how one might look:

Jacobson & Healey, Inc.

Office Manager/Accounting

Job Location:
McLean, VA

Qualifications:
Minimum of three to four years of experience in a position that relates to Office Management/Accounting. Must have a bachelor's degree with concentration in business and/or accounting. Strong writing and communications skills are necessary. Proficiency in Great Plains accounting software is required.

Duties/Responsibilities:
Manage office operations and oversee employee medical, insurance, and payroll plans. Handle ordering of office supplies, monitor vendor and service contracts, coordinate filing systems, implement office policies and procedures, and oversee postal and delivery functions. Keep general books and records, perform allocations of various expenses, manage bank accounts, and keep detailed ledgers.

Compensation/Benefits:
Salary is $40,000-$50,000, depending on experience and qualifications.

How to Apply:
Please e-mail your resume to resumes@jhi.com
or
Visit our Web site at www.jhi.com for additional information and to apply
or
Send your resume to Jacobson & Healey, Inc, 200 Lenders Lane, McLean, VA 22102

Getting discovered on the Web

Many of the employment-related sites on the Internet maintain databases where you can store your resume for viewing by employers. Although all sites are different, most hold a resume in their databases for 3-12 months. In addition, they often permit you to update your employment information at any time during that period.

Storing your resume in an online database is an effective way to put your credentials into circulation. Employers all over the world have access to the document 24 hours a day, 7 days a week. While you're at work or on vacation, your resume is promoting your qualifications to employers that are trying to fill vacant positions. And best of all, you rarely encounter a fee if you want to take advantage of this service.

Employers, on the other hand, pay either to enter and search the database or to obtain a candidate's contact information, after his or her resume is identified as a match with their requirements for a specific job. Some of these databases contain fewer than 50 resumes, while the larger sites can hold hundreds of thousands or even millions of such documents.

Employers search the databases by specifying the knowledge, skills, and experience they seek in a candidate. These search criteria are called "keywords." The computer reads through every resume in its database and identifies those with terms that match the specified keywords. The employer can then review each of the resumes and select specific individuals to contact for further evaluation.

DEVELOPING AN INTERNET-READY VERSION OF YOUR RESUME

The Internet is clearly an important way to connect with employers trying to fill their open positions. Your resume is the principal vehicle for making those connections, and you must design it especially to accomplish this task.

In order to respond to the jobs that employers post at employment-related Web-sites, your resume has to be able to travel over the Internet. In almost every case, your resume will make this journey in the form of e-mail. However, the technology that makes e-mail messages possible doesn't work well with resumes created with conventional word processing software. Therefore, to ensure that your resume arrives at its intended destination without being garbled, you need to reconfigure it for e-mail transmission and receipt.

The same requirement also applies when you enter your resume into an online resume database. Although some sites still accept and process paper resumes, most now require that you complete a form provided at their site or send in your resume via e-mail. Further, you may have to revise the content of your resume to ensure that the computer can find it in the database when your qualifications match the requirements for an available position. Otherwise, you will have successfully sent your resume over the Internet, only to have it overlooked after it arrives at its destination.

Revising the format of your resume

The formatting and organizational conventions used in your print resume may look great, but they're not going to survive a trip by e-mail. Creating an Internet resume requires attention to the following four key areas:

- The way information is organized and structured
- The way information is emphasized
- The length of the lines of text in your resume
- The kind of bullets you use to highlight your accomplishments

You first need to alter the way information is organized and structured in your resume. When you create a resume in a word processing program, you arrange information in paragraphs using indenting, tabs, and other conventions to make it more readable. E-mail does not recognize these devices, so you must eliminate them from your resume.

1. To eliminate the formatting in your resume, open the document on your computer.
2. Click on the File function on your tool bar and then select Save As.
3. In the Save As Type drop down list, select ASCII (American Standard Code for Information Interchange), Text Only, or Rich Text Format.
4. Click Save and your resume will be reproduced as an unformatted page of information. The resulting document doesn't look like much to the human eye, but the Internet loves it.

You also need to alter the way you emphasize the information on your resume. Most people use underlining and boldface type to emphasize certain points on their resumes. But e-mail cannot translate these flourishes, so you need to eliminate them in an Internet resume. To denote emphasis, capitalize all of the letters in such words and phrases.

⚑ *Red Flag*

Don't overuse all caps. In most cases, you should limit all caps to YOUR NAME and the following principal section headings:

- OBJECTIVE
- PROFILE
- EXPERIENCE
- EDUCATION
- PROFESSIONAL AFFILIATIONS & AWARDS

In a chronological and hybrid resume, use all caps for the titles of the positions you've held. In a functional and hybrid resume, capitalize your highlighted skills and abilities.

H Helpful Hint

You should also adjust the length of the lines of text in your resume. Most e-mail readers are set at a width of 60–65 characters. Lines of text that run longer than that are almost always garbled as these readers cannot implement the line wrapping function used in word processing systems. To ensure that your text gets read accurately, therefore, you must "slim down" the unformatted version of your resume. Count the characters in each line and insert a hard carriage break—end the line by using the Enter key on your keyboard—at or before the 65-character limit. It's a tedious process and creates an odd-looking document, but by completing this step, you'll know that your resume can be read by almost all e-mail systems.

Finally, you should also be careful about the kind of figures you use to highlight your accomplishments because e-mail readers don't recognize bullets. Therefore, use the + sign followed by two spaces to create a bulletlike effect on your Internet resume. For example:

+   Reduced overhead by 24% in less than 18 months.

Changing the content of your resume

Your resume's next step—after safely traveling through the Internet—is likely to be its processing into a computerized database. As with the resume management systems described in Chapter 8, these online databases hold information on a large number of candidates. To find the resumes of qualified individuals, recruiters must use keywords or search criteria to describe to a search engine the specific characteristics they seek. The search engine probes the database for resumes containing words that match those criteria.

Computers can't read between the lines or make assumptions about information that your resume is missing. Computers can only make comparisons and identify *exact matches* with the terms that actually appear in the document. For example, if a recruiter uses the keywords "Human Resources Management" as the search criteria, the computer will find any resume with that precise term. The computer won't find resumes that:

- Have even the most simple variation in the term—Human Resource Management, for example
- Use a synonym—personnel administration, for example—even though both terms are often used interchangeably
- Misspell any of the keywords—Human Resources Managfement, for example.

Hence, the secret to creating an effective Internet resume is to include all of the possible keywords that recruiters may use to identify a candidate with your qualifications and experience. You also need to spell all of those words correctly. For additional information on how you can identify the best keywords for your resume, please see Chapter 8.

TRANSMITTING YOUR INTERNET RESUME

You can use your Internet resume to respond to job postings at commercial employment Web-sites and at an employer's own site. You can also use your Internet resume to enter your credentials in one or more online resume databases where employers and third-party recruiters can access them.

Responding to job postings

As you can see in the illustrative job posting in the previous section, most employers want you to send your resume by embedding it either in an online application form available at their Web sites or in an e-mail message.

When including your resume in an online application form, follow the directions that the employer provides and carefully proofread the final document before submitting it. When you send your resume by e-mail, always use the Internet version of that document and follow this three-step process:

1. Address your message exactly as directed in the posting. Identify the position in the subject line, using either its designated requisition number or the position title the employer used in the posting.
2. Cut and paste your resume into the body of the e-mail message, using the appropriate functions on your computer's toolbar.

▶ *Red Flag*

It's best not to send your resume as an attachment unless the employer specifically asks that you do so. Most Human Resource Departments do not open attachments as they are the principal way computer viruses are spread over the Internet. Hence, a resume sent as an attachment is often deleted without any notification to the sender.

3. Proofread your message. It's actually best to perform two checks before you send your message. First, use the spell checker function on your computer to check for spelling and typographical errors before you cut and paste it into the message. Second, carefully proof-read the entire document to make sure that nothing was lost or mis-placed after it has been embedded in the e-mail message.

Once this process is complete, click the Send button on your e-mail program and your resume will begin its journey through cyberspace.

Putting your resume in an online database

Most commercial recruitment Web-sites provide detailed instructions for submitting a resume. In many cases, the instructions are very similar to the procedures used in responding to a job posting. The instructions on the Web-site will direct you either to cut and paste your resume into an online application form or to send your resume, embedded in an e-mail message, to a designated e-mail address.

After you complete the steps for posting a resume at the commercial Web-site, wait 48 hours and then search the database to see if you can find your resume.

- If you locate your resume, review it carefully to see if any errors occurred in transmission or processing. If you need to make corrections, follow the procedures for doing so that are provided on the site.
- If you cannot locate your resume, contact the site using the e-mail address provided for assistance and questions. In your message, provide your name as it appears on your resume, the date it was sent to the site, and the name of your e-mail service provider. In most cases, Web-site managers quickly resolve such situations.

Protecting your privacy

Sending your resume over the Internet to an employer's designated e-mail address is a personal and private communication. Hence, the employer is not likely to share the document with anyone outside the organization.

Storing your resume in an online resume database, on the other hand, puts that document and the information it contains into the public domain. Your resume is open and available to anyone with access to the database, and in the case of most commercial employment sites, that is any individual or organization paying the access fee—including your current employer.

▶ *Red Flag*

Although some sites provide a way to block certain organizations from viewing your resume, these systems are not foolproof. After your resume is entered in such a database, there is a high probability that other sites may copy it and reproduce in their databases. As a result, there is no fail-safe way to protect the confidentiality of your employment record after you store it online. It is also difficult to prevent an outdated version of your resume from circulating on the Internet forever.

You can do two things to protect yourself:

- Always date your Internet resume so that employers can quickly determine if they are reviewing a current or older version of your employment information.
- Remove your home address and telephone number from your resume and replace them with an e-mailbox that you use only for employment matters and a cell phone number. Check both frequently, so that you can respond quickly to employer inquiries.

An Internet resume is, without question, an unusual looking document. Despite its appearance, however, it is a useful document that can help you take advantage of the Internet's resources for finding a new or better job and managing your career.

Review

Use this WEDDLE's WIZNotes Review to evaluate what you've learned in this book and to build your confidence in writing a resume that will serve you well. After you work through the review questions, the problem-solving exercises, and the practice projects, you'll know exactly what you've learned and what you may need to review in order to write a great resume.

Q & A

1. All resumes should include:
   a. Contact information
   b. A description of your workplace experience
   c. Your accomplishments at work
   d. All of the above

2. If your career has progressed steadily through a series of ever more responsible positions, the best resume style for you is:
   a. Chronological.
   b. Functional.
   c. Hybrid.
   d. It doesn't really matter.

3. A Profile
   a. Appears at the end of your resume
   b. Describes the kind of employer for which you want to work
   c. Summarizes your key skills, abilities, experience, and knowledge
   d. Can be omitted if you are a recent college graduate.

4. When writing an Objective statement, you should be specific and include:
   a. The title of the job you're seeking
   b. The kind of place you like to work
   c. The benefit(s) you expect to deliver to your employer
   d. All of the above.

5. An electronic resume:
  a. Is designed for transmission over the Internet
  b. Cannot be reproduced on paper
  c. Does not include underlining or italics
  d. Works best when produced with 10-point type

Answers: (1)—d, (2)—a, (3)—c, (4)—d, (5)—c

Scenario:

1. Your employer has just announced that it is downsizing and that your position will be eliminated. You don't have an up-to-date resume and, therefore, can't apply for open positions you see advertised in the newspaper and on the Internet. Your first step is to

_____

_____ .

2. You decide to use the Internet to search for employment opportunities. You select a Web-site where you can view job postings and apply online. Before visiting the site, however, you must make several adjustments to your resume. These include

_____

_____ .

3. You left your last position following a dispute with your supervisor. The best way to handle this situation when writing your resume is

_____

_____ .

Answers: (1) determine your employment Objective. This statement will help you to develop a resume with a clear and compelling message about the kind of job you want and your qualifications for such a position. (2) Eliminating all word processing formats, placing selected words in all capital letters for emphasis, shortening the length of text lines, and ending them with a hard carriage return and using plus signs (+) to introduce bullets. (3) to omit it. Potentially negative information is best addressed in an interview, where you should be as straightforward and factual as possible; do not criticize your previous employer or supervisor.

Visual Test

1. Review the following excerpt from the Experience section of a resume.

    I was responsible for overseeing all sales activities performed by a field team of six agents. Hence, I was accountable for their daily sales performance, lead generation, and account management. My other responsibilities included agent training and development, monthly sales report preparation, key account management, and strategic planning.

2. What is the primary flaw in this section?
    a. It describes the person's tasks in a laundry list with little detail.
    b. It uses responsibility statements rather than action verbs to describe what tasks the person performed.
    c. It is too short and provides too little information for an employer to evaluate the person's capabilities.
    d. There is too much use of the pronoun "I."

Answer: b.

Consider This

Did you know that there are free job search features—called job agents—at many of today's job boards. These job agents enable you to specify the kind of job you want and then have the site search for matches. When a match is found, the site will notify you with a confidential e-mail message. Hence, job agents take a lot of the work out of looking for a job online, and they protect your privacy. You'll find job agents at such sites as:

*   www.careerbuilder.com
*   www.careerjournal.com
*   www.flipdog.com
*   www.hotjobs.com
*   www.monster.com

Please note: WEDDLE's has no financial or other interest in the above sites and their listing in this book is not an endorsement by WEDDLE's.

Practice Project

1. Schedule a performance appraisal with yourself, every six months.
2. Use your resume to evaluate your progress in advancing your career.

    - If you have participated in a training program or gained important new experience, update your resume to reflect that additional capability.
    - If, on the other hand, you have failed to acquire new skills or experience, your inability to add any new information to your resume will reflect that lack of progress and signal that your career may be falling behind.

3. In either case, set specific goals for the next six months to help you to gain new qualifications that you can then add to your resume.

WEDDLE's WIZNotes
Resource Center

The learning you've done about resume writing and job search doesn't need to stop here. The WIZNotes Resource Center list other books and publications that will help you find a new or better job and manage your career successfully. Look for these resources at your favorite bookstore or local library and at the WEDDLE's Web-site at **http://www.weddles .com**. Stop by and visit us today.

WEDDLE's Publications

Career Fitness A philosophy of working and a regimen of job search and career management techniques that will build up both the paycheck and the satisfaction you bring home from the office each day.

WEDDLE's 2005/6 Guide to Employment Web Sites The "consumer's report" of job boards: provides detailed information on 350 of the best job boards covering all major occupations and industries.

WEDDLE's 2005/6 Guide to Association Web Sites A guide to the employment-related resources at the Web-sites of over 1,800 professional associations and societies.

WEDDLE's 2005/6 Directory of Employment-Related Internet Sites The "address book" of job boards, listing over 8,000 sites, organized by career field, industry and geographic focus.

WEDDLE's WizNotes: Fast Facts on Job Boards The "CliffsNotes" of job boards, each volume provides detailed information on the job boards for a specific career field or employment situation.

- Sales/Marketing
- Finance/Accounting
- Engineers
- Managers/Executives
- Recent College Grads
- Human Resources
- Finding a Job on the Web
- Writing a Great Resume

Send Us Your Favorite Tips

In your quest for learning, have you ever experienced that sublime moment when you figure out a trick that saves you time or trouble? Perhaps you realized that what was taking ten steps could be done in two . . . if you just did something a little differently. Or you found a little-known technique that gets great results. Whatever it is, your discovery works and it's helpful.

If you've discovered such a tip and you'd like to share it with others, the WEDDLE's staff would love to hear from you. Go to our Web site at **http://www.weddles.com** and click on the Contact Us link at the bottom of our Home Page. If your tip has general applicability, we will publish it as part of our *free* e-mail newsletter for job seekers and career activists. To receive this monthly publication (which covers tips for finding a new or better job online and managing your career successfully), simply go to WEDDLE's Web-site and sign up at the spinning globe on our Home Page.

INDEX

T

templates for resume development, 44–45
text boxes, 111
titling your resume, 37
typeface, 44, 110

U

underlining, 111
Unisex Edition of the ACT
 Interest Inventory (UNI-
 ACT), 49
university degree acronyms, 62,
 74, 86, 98, 115
USAJOBS, 118

V

VetJobs.com, 118
vocabulary. *See also* content
 action verbs, 43, 64, 76, 89,
 100, 129
 keywords, 111–113, 123
 recruiter's, 27
Vocational Interest Inventory
 (VII), 49
volunteer work, 96

Y

Yahoo! HotJobs, 118

NOTES